Troubl

Also by Judith M. Berrisford

SUE'S CIRCUS HORSE
PONIES ALL SUMMER
PONY FOREST ADVENTURE

Judith M. Berrisford

Trouble at Ponyways

Illustrations by Elisabeth Grant

DRAGON
GRANADA PUBLISHING
London Toronto Sydney New York

Published by Granada Publishing Limited
in Dragon Books 1977

ISBN 0 583 30245 9

First published in Great Britain by
University of London Press Ltd 1959

Granada Publishing Limited
Frogmore, St Albans, Herts AL2 2NF
and
3 Upper James Street, London W1R 4BP
1221 Avenue of the Americas, New York, NY 10020 USA
117 York Street, Sydney, NSW 2000, Australia
100 Skyway Avenue, Toronto, Ontario, Canada M9W 3A6
Trio City, Coventry Street, Johannesburg 2001, South Africa
CML Centre, Queen & Wyndham, Auckland 1, New Zealand

Made and printed in Great Britain by
Richard Clay (The Chaucer Press) Ltd
Bungay, Suffolk
Set in Linotype Plantin

CONTENTS

CHAPTER I

MIKE'S WIFE

'Mr Dashmore!' Toni called as she walked through the open door of Ponyways and put down her suitcase in the hall. 'Are you there, Mr Dashmore? Hey, Mike!'

Her cousin, Rosemary, looked at the sporting prints on the walls, and the rosettes tacked on the wood panelling of the stairways. Ponyways! It was good to be back here again.

Ponyways was the home of Mike Dashmore, the international show-jumping star. It was a country house, set amid paddocks and meadows, in a southern county where the downs billowed to the sea. From the front door Rosemary could see perfect riding country, and, between a gap in the hills, the English Channel, only a mile away, calm today, with a blue-sailed yacht dipping round a red marker buoy.

'There's nowhere quite like Ponyways,' Toni said, echoing Rosemary's thoughts. 'Isn't it bliss to be back for another summer holiday?'

'Yes, we're lucky.'

Rosemary nodded. The young people who came to Ponyways from all over Britain every year were glad there was such a place where they could stay with a top-flight show-jumper, popular Mike Dashmore, and take part in his holiday courses with lots of riding and mounted activity.

'I wonder where Mike is,' Toni murmured, going back to the front door. 'In the stables I suppose.'

'Hullo, you two!' The kitchen door swung open, and a fair-haired girl ran to meet the two cousins, plaits flying. 'It's lovely to see you again.'

'Rather!' came a boy's voice from behind her. 'How's tricks?'

'Hullo, Fay! Hullo, Dave!'

Toni and Rosemary Brooke greeted Fay Wood and her young brother whom they had not seen since their summer holidays at Ponyways last year.

'Where's Pete?' asked Toni.

'I'm here in the kitchen,' called Fay's elder brother, through the open doorway from the background. 'I'm making sure that the sausages don't burn while you and Fay exchange girlish greetings. Hurry, if you want some lunch. We've cooked lashings.'

'Wizard!' Toni led the dash to the table. 'I'm ravenous!'

'Sausages and mash,' said Rosemary appreciatively, and looked round the kitchen. 'But where's our illustrious host?'

'And his wife,' added Toni. 'Don't forget Mike married a couple of months ago.'

'Wedding bells! And wedded bliss!' said Rosemary. 'And thank everyone's lucky stars that he married a horsewoman.'

'She's still jumping under her maiden name of Norma Gill,' put in Fay. 'And she's doing well, too. She won the Jupiter Stakes last year and came second in the Mallard Cup.'

'With two champion show-jumpers to run Ponyways,' said sandy-haired Pete, 'the holiday-course should be more worthwhile than ever.'

'But where are the happy bride and groom now?' persisted Toni. 'And – more important, since I'm feeling so hungry, where are Mrs Roylance and Maud?'

'Goodness knows,' Dave shrugged as he speared a sausage with his fork. 'But I'm sure they'd want us to have a good feed.'

'Yes, that's what they must have intended because they left the sausages on the scullery table,' said Fay. 'Now where have they all vanished to? I mean bride, groom, cook and help – not the sausages.'

'Perhaps they're all out on a picnic ride,' suggested Rosemary, helping herself to the rapidly-disappearing feast.

'Not Mrs Roylance and Maud!' Toni laughed at the thought of Mike's plump housekeeper and her thin, nervy, disaster-predicting sister astride any of the Ponyways mounts.

'It's probably their day off,' said Fay.

'That's more likely,' Toni agreed. She took another mouthful of sausage and mash. 'Mmm! Delicious! I never knew you could cook so well, Fay.'

Fay smiled and glanced at her two brothers.

'I had some capable help,' she admitted.

'I peeled three potatoes,' boasted Dave.

'And I set the table and stopped the sausages being burned while you three girls were gurgling around,' Pete said.

'What's for pudding?' asked Dave.

'Apples, I should think,' said Fay. 'There's half-a-barrel full in the pantry.'

'Sssh!' Toni broke off, listening to the sound of hooves on the gravel. 'The others are back.'

'We'll clear the table,' Rosemary said, starting to stack the plates, 'just in case they haven't had a picnic after all, and want to have their lunch in here.'

'Good idea!' Pete stood up and began to collect the knives and forks. 'We can eat our apples afterwards while we look at the ponies.'

'I hope Mike's still got Russet.' Fay's eyes were dreamy as she thought about the chestnut mare she had ridden during her last summer's stay at Ponyways. 'She's a grand jumper.' She looked out of the window. 'Here come some of the others. They're taking the ponies round to the loose boxes. I can't see Mike.'

Just then a shadow fell across the threshold.

'Hul-*lo*!' Fay looked up to stare at a good-looking, yellow-haired boy, who had come in through the back doorway. 'Were you out with the riders who've just rolled up?'

The boy stood for a moment, looking slim and elegant. Then he shook his head, smiled absently and wandered through the kitchen to the panelled sitting-room which Mike Dashmore used as an office and study.

'Who's he?' Toni looked enquiringly at Pete.

'Search me. I've never seen him before.' Pete turned to follow the stranger. 'I'll find out whether he wants anything.'

He opened the office door and put his head round. 'Are you looking for something?' he asked. Next moment he turned to face the other four in surprise. 'There's nobody here!' he told them. 'He's vanished!'

'But the boy came in here.' Toni pushed past him into the room. 'I saw him.'

'So did I,' Fay looked round the room, puzzled. Her glance fell on the garden door in the far wall of the office. 'He must have gone straight out on to the lawn,' she guessed. 'Odd!'

Pete looked baffled as he crossed to the window and craned out to try to get a glimpse of the returning riders who were now out of sight behind the loose boxes. 'I say, I do hope Mike's got some new horses,' he said. 'I'm getting too big for the ponies. I've been riding Diamond at Captain Crabb's at home and he's quite fifteen-two.'

'Samba for me,' stocky, young Dave said, loyal to the black Exmoor.

'Catkin's fast.' Toni's brown eyes were warm as she thought about the grey mare. 'And she's so gentle. She jumped almost five feet last year, and she's super at dressage.'

'I wish I rode as well as you do, Toni.' Fay gazed at her friend admiringly. Then she smiled. 'But I'll never be an expert. All I ask is to ride a quiet, sensible pony like Russet.'

They stopped talking as the kitchen door opened, and in trooped the riders who had just ridden up the drive. First, there was a rather plain girl, Liz Stratton, with mousy hair and spectacles who seemed to be the eldest. Then there was a jolly-looking girl with wavy auburn hair; a pretty dark girl who was well turned-out, and two quite young boys who were obviously twins. The boys had tawny, curly hair and freckles. They looked as if they could be mischievous, but just now their faces were glum. In fact all the riders looked tired and hungry, and – thought Toni – strangely scared.

'Is anything wrong?' asked Toni.

'As wrong as it could be!' Liz Stratton, the girl with pink-rimmed spectacles, spoke for them all. 'Mike's just broken his leg.'

'Broken his leg!' Toni echoed, numbed. 'How did that happen?'

'You might well ask!' Cherry Wain, the pretty dark girl turned to Rosemary, Toni, Fay, Pete and Dave who were listening in shocked silence. 'We were riding along the sands when Mike's wife suggested that we took the track up to the headland.'

'We did that,' added the girl with auburn hair, 'and rode across country, jumping everything we met. Then we came to a big earth wall with a gorse hedge on top. Mike Dashmore told us to miss that one, and go through the gate instead.'

'But that wife of his,' Liz cut in, her eyes flashing indignantly behind her spectacles, 'wouldn't listen to him. She wanted to jump it, of course, just to show us yet again what a marvellous rider she is, as if we didn't already know!'

'So Mike said "very well" he'd give her a lead,' prompted Molly, the auburn-haired girl. 'But she wouldn't let him.'

'She called him back,' said George Jollison. 'And I don't think he heard.'

'He couldn't have,' agreed Gerry, the other Jollison twin, ' 'cos he kept right on. That made Mrs Dashmore mad,' he added, 'and she rode after him.'

'Yes, and she cut right across,' Liz explained. 'She jumped a moment ahead of Mike. He hadn't a chance to pull up. Destiny tried to swerve, but she hadn't an earthly. They collided in mid-air. Destiny came down in the ditch and rolled on Mike breaking his leg.'

'While Norma's mare just pecked and recovered,' Molly ended.

'Was Destiny hurt?' Pete asked quickly. He remembered Mike's big grey mare from last year. He had also watched her on the television screen.

'Luckily, no,' said Liz. 'Small thanks to Norma. I've never seen a more criminal piece of bad riding and sheer bad sportsmanship.'

'Oh, drop it, Liz.' Cherry sighed. 'That's no way to talk of Mike's wife!'

'I suppose not,' agreed Liz. 'But I'm flaming. I've got to let fly, or I'll burst. Norma Dashmore's a spoiled, lazy, show-off. Look how perfect things were here before Mike married her. You all know how grand it was last year when Mike ran the place with Mrs Roylance and Maud. Why he had to pick Norma as a bride—' She broke off. 'I suppose I'd better dry up before someone accuses me of being jealous.'

There was an awkward silence.

'Where's Mrs Roylance?' Toni said, tactfully trying to change the subject.

'Norma sacked her!' Molly announced.

'Yes. Norma said she was going to get some proper staff,' Liz added, 'who would run the place like clockwork. But of course she hasn't been able to get anyone at all. You know what it's like these days.'

'Where's Mike now?' Rosemary asked.

'In Drayfield Hospital,' said Molly. 'We phoned for an ambulance. Norma went with him, and we brought back the animals.'

Animals! Toni jerked as she suddenly remembered the dogs – the two golden retrievers who had been there last summer.

'Where are Candy and Floss?'

'In their run, most likely. Oh no, they're not. They've just walked in!' Gerry Jollison said, and added, at a tangent. 'Gosh, I'm hungry!'

'We'll get you people some lunch,' Fay offered.

'We'll help.' Cherry took off her jacket and hung it carefully over the back of a chair before taking down a gay check apron from a peg behind the door and tying it round her waist. 'Keeping busy will stop us brooding over poor old Mike.'

What a fate for the man who had been their hero for years! Liz thought as she helped the others. A bride like Norma – and now a broken leg!

While the others ate their lunch, Toni, Rosemary, Fay, Dave and Pete munched apples on the window seat and fondled the lovable, sentimental retrievers. Liz thought how she and the others had come to Ponyways to have a grand pony-holiday. What a good time they would have with the ponies if only Mike hadn't broken his leg! It must be dreary for him in Drayfield hospital, wondering how they were all going on; perhaps fretting about the animals and how they would be looked after. It would be wretched for anyone as active as Mike to have his leg in plaster and be out of the saddle for weeks. Poor Mike!

'I must try to like Norma!' Liz told herself. 'For Mike's sake.'

Meanwhile Toni was wondering what Norma was really like? Was she as spoiled and selfish as Liz made out?

Fifteen minutes later as they were all helping to wash and dry the dishes and put away the crockery, they heard a car on the gravel.

'Here comes Mike's wife,' Liz said bitterly.

Through the open door at the end of the hall they saw Norma Dashmore, immaculately booted and breeched, step from a shiny, black car.

'Thank you so much, Dr Southcott,' she was saying to the driver. 'You're an angel to go so far out of your way.'

'Not at all, my dear.' The elderly doctor raised his hat. 'I couldn't have you waiting about catching buses – not after all you've been through.'

As the car drove away Norma Dashmore came across the drive towards the front door. She certainly looked pale, Toni thought, watching her mount the steps, or was that just the effect of her black jacket and bowler against her fair skin?

'So you're the new arrivals?' Norma's dark lashes swept up from her gentian-blue eyes as she took in Toni, Rosemary, Fay, Pete and Dave. 'I'm so sorry you didn't have a real welcome.'

'Don't worry about that, Mrs Dashmore,' Fay said. 'How's Mike – I mean, Mr Dashmore?'

'Well, his leg's been set,' said Mike Dashmore's young bride. 'Luckily it was a clean break below the knee. He'll be home in a few days. First he'll be in a wheelchair and then on crutches.'

'On crutches!' Pete echoed feelingly. 'Oh, gosh!'

All eyes turned again to Mike's wife as she suddenly sank into one of the high-backed tapestry chairs in the hall.

'Goodness! I feel quite odd.' She passed a hand over her forehead and tilted back her bowler. A strand of ash-blonde hair fell across her face.

'I expect it's the shock.' Fay was sympathetic and capable

as always. 'Let me make you a cup of tea.'

'That really would be quite, quite angelic of you.' Norma Dashmore managed a weak, but nevertheless dazzling, smile. 'So thoughtful! But do you think you could make it coffee – quite black? You'll find the coffeepot on the kitchen dresser.' She stood up, faltered for a moment, put a hand on the back of the chair for support and turned to the stairs. 'I'll go and change now. When I come down we'll all have a talk. Goodness knows how we're going to manage to run Ponyways, or even keep it open. What with Mike in hospital, and no cook, no maid, and no help in the stables. The only solution may be – no guests!'

CHAPTER II

WILLING PONIES – AND OTHERS

Half an hour later, wearing a turquoise linen blouse and well-fitting navy slacks, Norma Dashmore sat at the kitchen table, smoking a cigarette in between sipping coffee.

'So you've been talking it over. I thought you might,' Norma was saying. 'You don't want to be sent home in the middle of your holiday. And so you're all ready to do your share of the work. Well, I call that a very fair offer, and I'm going to take you up on it. Now who's going to do what?'

'Fay's a good cook,' said Toni, 'and Rosemary and I can help her in the kitchen.'

'Right!' Norma nodded briskly. 'Then that's settled. Now what about the stable work? Cherry!' She turned to dark-haired Cherry Wain. 'This is where you shine. I'll leave it to you to organize a team of helpers. Carry on with the usual routine. Bed the beasts down. Don't forget the ten o'clock feed. Oh, and we'll have that tack cleaned, please. Muck-out, and groom tomorrow morning. Work out the exercising schedule among yourselves, and if you want any help over anything come straight to me.'

'Where shall we find you, Mrs Dashmore?' Liz asked. 'What will you be doing?'

'Well, of course, I shall be at the hospital with Mike quite a lot,' Norma said, stubbing out her cigarette and walking to the door. 'And I shall have my hands full schooling Destiny for him. I'm going to have a look at her now.'

It was good to be in the Ponyways stables again, Toni decided. She hummed to herself as, later that afternoon, she carried fresh straw for bedding into Catkin's box. The grey mare seemed to remember her from last summer. She nuzzled Toni's shoulder when the girl made much of her. Then, as a last year's joke came to the mare's mind, she nuzzled at Toni's pocket for the apple which Toni had not forgotten to hide.

While Catkin crunched her apple, Toni spread out the deep straw bedding and contentedly sniffed the smell of pony and stables.

'Well, what do you make of her?' Rosemary asked.

Toni pushed back her curly hair and turned to face her cousin who had come into the loose box.

'She remembered me right away.' Toni slapped Catkin's quarters in a friendly way. 'Get over, pony.' She turned back to Rosemary. 'She even remembered to look for her apple.'

'Not Catkin, stupid.' Rosemary gave her pony-bemused cousin a pitying look. 'I mean Mike's wife.'

'Oh, her! Well, she's certainly wonderful to look at,' Toni said after a moment's thought. 'She looked terrific in that black jacket and white stock. And those boots! No mud, and not a hair out of place after all she'd been through.'

'After all Mike had been through,' Rosemary corrected softly and then added: 'Ah well, I suppose Norma had quite a shock, and I'm sure none of us minds buckling-to during the crisis.' She looked across at Toni and Catkin. 'She's a super mare, isn't she? And not a bit *small* for you. She must be quite fourteen-two. Now Star seems suddenly *short*, this year,' Rosemary confided mournfully. 'I've grown, of course – suddenly shot up, as Daddy says. I'll have to change to one of the bigger ponies.'

'Then Dave can ride Star,' Toni said. 'That will soften his disappointment. I don't know if he's discovered the fact yet, but George Jollison's riding Samba.'

'Hey, you two!' Cherry's head came round the door. 'Get moving! We've masses to do before tea-time, and Fay's sure to need some help with the cooking later. Break up the gossip session and lend a hand with the tack.'

The tack-room seemed too small for everybody to work in

at one and the same time so Toni collected a couple of bridles and took them into the yard to share a bucket of water and a tin of saddle-soap with Pete and Dave.

She was sponging the leather when Fay came across from the kitchen, carrying a pair of black riding boots.

'Oh, Toni,' she greeted her friend. 'Mrs Dashmore said would I be "a darling" and find somebody to clean these. But you're busy, I see, Toni. What about you, Dave?'

'Those boots don't look dirty to me,' Dave said guardedly.

'But she was wearing them today,' Fay told her brother. 'And she's got to be properly turned out for the sake of Ponyways' reputation.'

'I still don't see why she can't clean her own boots,' Dave said. 'I don't mind cleaning saddles, but Mrs Dashmore's boots! – well, I think that's the limit. Oh, all right. Hand them over.'

'Hey, Fay,' said Pete. 'What's going on in the kitchen?'

'Yes, what's for tea?' asked Dave.

'Baked beans on toast,' said Fay, 'and I thought I'd make some pancakes.'

'Oh, you'll be ready for me to help you now,' said Toni. She linked her arm through Fay's. 'Lead on, O Chef! What's my line? I'm an expert pancake-batter-beaterer!'

Next morning Toni was up early to tackle the breakfast-getting with Fay. Liz and Molly also helped. Rosemary and her brothers were in the stables, feeding, mucking-out and grooming with the Jollison twins under Cherry's efficient directions.

In the kitchen Candy and Floss, the two golden retrievers, did not make breakfast-getting any easier.

'Look out, Floss!' Fay just missed tripping over the dog as she carried a cup of tea to the door.

'Don't say you're taking that up to Norma!' Liz's eyebrows rose above her spectacle rims. 'Let her come down for it like the rest of us. After all we're supposed to be paying guests – not unpaid minions.'

'If only we were all as naturally sweet and unselfish as Fay is,' Toni sighed as Fay trudged upstairs with the cup of tea, 'then, oh! – what a wonderful world it would be.'

She turned over the fifteenth slice of toast and broke the tenth egg into the frying pan.

'Fay always was too kind-hearted,' Toni went on. 'She was just the same last year. If ever there was a dull job, Fay offered to take it on. She just couldn't bear to see anybody else have to do it. Not that there were many dull jobs with Mike here.'

'Nor much housework with Mrs Roylance and Maud,' said Molly, spooning marmalade into a big glass dish.

'Mike had everything running so smoothly,' said Liz. Her brown eyes blinked behind her spectacles. 'I keep on thinking about him. Poor man! I wonder if he's worrying how we're all carrying on without him. Hullo!' She turned as Fay breathlessly came back into the kitchen. 'What now, saint?'

'Mrs Dashmore doesn't feel like coming down,' Fay said, taking a tray from a shelf. 'She was very sweet about it. She said she hated to give so much trouble. A slice of toast and some butter and marmalade would do, but could I be an angel and take it upstairs?'

'Oh well,' Liz shrugged. 'It seems you've got to learn the hard way!'

'I expect Mrs Dashmore's upset about Mike,' said Toni. 'After all he is her husband, and he has broken his leg and she must love him.'

'Norma Dashmore loves only one person – herself!' Liz said with bitter certainty. 'If she cared two hoots about Mike she'd be down here, taking charge, making a go of things. I know her type. She gets through life the easy way. So long as some other mug will do the work, why should she bother? That's her motto. She may be a marvellous show-jumper, but in everything else she's just a flop.'

'Hey, tone it down, Liz,' Toni advised. 'She'll hear.'

'I don't care!' Liz flashed. 'Oh, how I long to tell her just what I think of her!'

After breakfast and the washing-up, Cherry wiped her hands on the roller towel and looked out of the window to see white puffs of clouds scudding in from the sea.

'It's a lovely morning,' she said. 'Who's for a ride?'

'Count me out,' said Liz. 'I've got to write a letter home. I haven't had a chance for the last few days.'

'We've lots of things to fetch from the village,' said Fay. 'We're almost out of cornflakes, and I expect we ought to order some meat.'

'Suppose Rosemary and Fay and I do the shopping,' suggested Toni.

'And the rest of us will go up on the Downs,' Cherry decided. 'We'll give the ponies a gallop and get back early to help you with lunch.'

They went to the stables and began to saddle-up, singing the Ponyways trail song, an old cowboy hit-tune that Mike had parodied:

'Get along little pony, get along,
Take me up on the Downs where I belong.'

'Hold everything!' George, elder of the Jollison twins by half an hour, ran up to them.

'What's wrong?' Cherry paused with her foot in the stirrup.

'I went to fetch Brandy,' George gasped, 'and Mrs Dashmore was in the paddock on Destiny. She called to me, and said she wanted three volunteers to raise the jumps. She's already been round twice.'

'She can count me out,' Pete gathered up Sultan's reins.

'I don't mind staying,' said Dave. 'I'd like to see Mrs Dashmore jump.'

'I'll make up the threesome,' volunteered Gerry Jollison, going to his twin's side.

'You see!' Toni turned to Fay as they started off with Rosemary and the ponies for the village. 'Norma Dashmore staged a quick recovery as soon as the housework was done. You know, I'm coming round to Liz's way of thinking. I've got a nasty feeling that Norma's going to make use of us all to get the house and stables run as easily as possible without having to lift a finger herself! And, oh goodness! – I wonder if she only married Mike so that she could use the Ponyways' horses to further her show-jumping ambitions! Poor, poor Mike.'

CHAPTER III

LIZ BOILS OVER

The ponies were alert and playing with their bits. Catkin cocked back an ear and tossed his head as the tang of salt came to his nostrils. Russet danced sideways across the lane when they entered the village of Marling.

'Cooo-eee!'

Toni's eyes lit up as she recognized the call of Mrs Roylance, the former cook at Ponyways. She could see Mrs Roylance's cottage-loaf shape. Her body was like two round cobs, one on top of the other. Her head, with its bun of hair, made two more 'rounds', comfortable and homely as she waddled down the path of one of the cottages.

Rosemary waved. 'Hullo, Mrs Roylance,' she called.

''Ow are you all?' Mrs Roylance ledged her plump arms on the top of the gate having put her hedge-clippers on the path. 'I thought I might be seeing some of you young ladies. I 'eard the 'ooves in the lane. "That's some of the young folk from Ponyways," I said to myself. So I thought I'd come out and give Fanny's 'edge a clip on the off-chance of having a word with you.' She paused for breath and went on to explain. 'Fanny's my friend. Me and Maud are stayin' with 'er a bit, since that saucy madam gave me the sack!' She glared indignantly, vaguely south-west, in the direction of Ponyways. ''Ow're you all gettin' on?'

'We're missing you, Mrs Roylance,' Toni said truthfully. 'There seems to be such a lot of housework.'

'I bet there is, ducks.' Somehow Mrs Roylance seemed pleased about this despite the fact that she nodded sympathetically. She gave a plump wriggle of pleasure as she adjusted the broad straps of her apron. 'An' I bet that there pert bit doesn't so much as lift 'er 'and. Pity Mr Mike 'ad to go and marry 'er.

Met 'er one week, married 'er the next almost. 'Ow is 'e?'

'Mike's had an accident,' Rosemary told her.

'Broken 'is leg!' Mrs Roylance echoed in dismay when they told her what had happened. 'Poor fellow! An' 'im always so nice, too. Always such a gentleman. Not that bein' in 'ospital won't give 'im a bit of a rest from *'er*.'

'Don't they get on well?' Rosemary couldn't resist asking.

'They gets on well enough, ducks,' Mrs Roylance said with some foreboding head-wags, 'but only becos 'e gives in to her. That's why. He can't see no wrong in 'er. An' of course she's clever. Sweet as 'oney she is when 'e's around. She twists 'im round 'er little finger. Deep as they make 'em, that one is.'

'Here's Maud,' Toni said as a tall, thin woman came round the corner.

'She's been a season, I must say.' Mrs Roylance bristled bossily as her sister pushed open the gate. 'Whatever 'ave you been doin', Maud? A full hour it's taken you, just to get that shoulder of lamb from the butcher's.'

'I met Mrs Baines. Poor thing!' Maud put down the shopping basket on the path. 'Bad bronchitis Mr Baines 'as got,' she reported. 'I don't like the sound of it at all. I wouldn't be surprised if 'e didn't last the week out an' that's a fact. A decline! That's what he's going into.'

'Get along with you, Maud,' Mrs Roylance scoffed. 'You'll be giving these young ladies the droops. Don't take no notice,' she warned the girls. 'When Maud says anyone won't last the week they're usually up and about next day. It's almost a good sign, as you might say.' She turned to her sister. 'Now these young ladies 'ave got some real bad news.' She paused to add drama to her announcement. 'Mr Mike's 'ad an accident – an' broke 'is leg!'

'Oh!' Maud clutched at the gate to support herself. 'I don't like the sound of that.' She listened anxiously while Toni briefly told her about the fall. ''E ought to be X-rayed all over, 'e did, just to be on the safe side. You never know with a fall like that. 'Specially with bein' rolled on an' all. 'E might 'ave done a lot more than broke 'is leg. Things wot won't show themselves yet awhile. Mr Keithley, down by the green, 'ad a fall like that. He thought 'e was all right.' She paused. 'Two weeks later 'e was in 'is box.'

'I'm sure Mike will be all right, Maud,' Rosemary assured her. 'He's being well looked after at the hospital.' She gathered up Catkin's reins. 'We must be going, Mrs Roylance. We've got to do the shopping for lunch.'

'I'm that sorry for you young ladies,' Mrs Roylance consoled. 'On 'oliday, and 'avin' to work as 'ard as you do at 'ome.'

'Why don't you come back and look after us, Mrs Roylance?' Fay suggested. 'I'm sure Mrs Dashmore didn't mean it when she sacked you.'

'Come back there? Work for *'er*?' Mrs Roylance's voice rose indignantly. 'Catch me!' She softened. 'I tell you what, though, I don't mind 'elpin' you young ladies. So if there's any washin' wants doin', or any mendin' or patchin', you just bring it down 'ere. Yes, I'd like to know how you all get on, so drop in from time to time.'

Meanwhile, at Ponyways, Liz was in the low-beamed sitting-room writing a letter. Her mother had died four years ago and, since then, Liz had helped a housekeeper to 'look after' her father who was the doctor in Whitethorn, a market town in Leicestershire. Liz got plenty of riding at home, but the highlight of her summer was to travel by train to Ponyways and spend a holiday there. Liz was seventeen now and had been at Ponyways for the last three summer holidays.

Always, when the time came to go, Liz wondered how she could ever leave her father. He would be so lonely without her, but he always insisted that she deserved a break from school and housework.

Most of the old crowd are back here at Ponyways, Daddy – she wrote. Then she looked up from her letter as the back door slammed. Next moment Gerry Jollison came bounding through the house.

'Hullo, Liz!' He burst into the room. 'Have you seen my crash cap?'

'I can't say I have, Gerry.' Liz looked surprised. 'I thought you'd gone with the others. Why aren't you on the Downs?'

'Didn't you know? Oh, of course, you were in here writing your letter.' Gerry began to explain. 'Mrs Dashmore got out of bed after she'd had her breakfast. She decided to school Destiny, and she wanted three of us to stay behind to raise the jumps.'

'And so?' Liz prompted.

'Well, we've raised the jumps to top height,' Gerry said. 'And Mrs Dashmore's told us that we may go. If you ask me she sent us away because Destiny was beginning to knock things down, and Mrs Dashmore didn't want to look a fool in front of us.'

'More than likely,' Liz nodded. 'So where are you going now?'

'Well, George and Dave and me thought we'd ride to the Downs after the others. Ah! Here's my cap.' He picked it up from under the sofa. 'See you later, Liz.'

' 'Bye,' Liz replied absently.

She glanced at the brass dial of the grandfather clock. It was a quarter past eleven. Norma had been schooling Destiny for almost two hours. No wonder Destiny was beginning to knock down the jumps. Temperamental Destiny was easily bored, and though she would jump almost endlessly when coaxingly handled by Mike, she would not take kindly to Norma's steam-roller methods of putting her over the same jumps all morning. It was a shame. Liz got up from her chair, and put the unfinished letter in her writing case. She went upstairs and paused on the first floor.

From the landing window she got a clear view of the paddock. She saw Norma swinging the mare round to put her at the triple-bars. One of the poles of the in-and-out was down, and the stile lay on its side. Destiny was tired. She trotted listlessly towards the jump.

Thwack! Norma's switch changed the trot to a weary canter. Destiny jumped carelessly. She caught the first bar of the triple with her hind legs, bringing down all three bars.

Norma reined-up and hit the mare. Then she rode her at the four-foot-high paddock fence which was made of solid oak rails. Destiny would not knock those if she could help it. They would hurt her too much. Norma realized it. Relentlessly she jumped the mare back and forth over the paddock fence. Destiny's neck and flanks were lathered with sweat. Her sensitive ears were back.

Liz did not wait to see any more. She ran downstairs, along the hall, out of the side door and along the path to the paddock. The mare was now playing-up, but not even Destiny could buck Norma off her back. Mike's wife was a fine horsewoman despite her ruthless tactics.

After a final plunge from the mare, Norma subdued her. She turned Destiny, and rode her back at the rails.

Destiny was tired now. Liz flinched when she heard her hind-legs catch the rail with a painful rap. Poor, poor Destiny. Liz ran faster as Norma turned the mare towards the made-up jumps. She would not risk a bad fall through Destiny hitting the fixed rails again. Whatever value she placed on horseflesh, Norma was always careful of her own skin. But she was going to teach Destiny – once and for all – that she was mistress. As long as there was a jump left standing in the paddock she was determined to put the mare over it.

Liz angrily hurried through the gateway into the paddock.

'Mrs Dashmore!' she called, unsuccessfully trying to keep her voice steady.

Norma reined in Destiny, and swung the mare round. She faced Liz with a calm smile.

'What is it, Liz?'

'I don't want to butt in, but I've been watching you jump Destiny.'

'Yes, Liz?' Norma Dashmore prompted and now her tone was honey-sweet.

'I think you're jumping her too hard,' Liz managed to say quickly.

'Really!' Norma Dashmore raised her eyebrows. 'Surely I'm the best judge of that. When you've had as much to do with horses as I have, you'll know that it doesn't do to let a mare have her own way. But if you're unhappy about her, by all means stay and see fair play.'

Liz stepped forward and grasped Destiny's bridle. She happened to touch the mare's sweat-lathered neck and she felt a pulse beating rapidly there. Destiny began to tremble.

'Please, Mrs Dashmore,' Liz pleaded. 'I can't bear to see Destiny driven too hard. Please, *please* don't jump her any more this morning.'

Norma's eyes showed impatience.

'That's quite enough, Liz,' she said firmly. 'I can't have you young people dictating to me. Now, with your permission, I'll carry on where I left off.'

Liz stood back. What should she do? Should she persuade herself that there was no need to interfere on Destiny's behalf? Or should she make another effort to stop Norma?

Liz turned away, wretched. She felt she was being a traitor to dear, loyal Destiny. Slowly she walked to the gate. She stopped as she heard the sound of Norma's switch against the mare's flanks, and the thud of hooves as Mike's wife put the mare at the first jump. Liz's breath caught. She heard Destiny land and canter towards the next jump. Again came the sound of the switch, followed by a sharp rap and the crash of a falling bar. Destiny had knocked down the jump. Norma's voice rose angrily, scolding the mare.

'You sulky animal.' Norma brought the switch down on Destiny's withers. 'I'll teach you.'

At that threat Liz acted. There was one way she could stop Norma forcing the mare over the jumps. She would knock them down. She ran to the nearest jump and pushed it over.

'Stop that, Liz!' shouted Norma.

Liz defiantly sped on, knocking down the poles and pushing over the brushwood fences until there was not one obstacle left over which Norma could force Destiny to jump.

She waited tensely while Norma rode up to her.

'What's the meaning of this, Liz?' Norma asked coldly.

'Isn't it obvious?' Liz faced her quietly.

She turned and quickly walked away. She was through the paddock gateway before she heard Norma's voice calling angrily after her.

'Liz! *Elizabeth!* Come back and put up these jumps.'

Liz shouted over her shoulder: 'Not on your life! And if you put them up, I'll knock them down again.'

She ran to the house, up the stairs and into her room. She felt appalled by what she had done. Suppose Norma sent her home in disgrace? She walked to the window. Norma was replacing the jumps. She put up the last pole and began to lead Destiny towards the stables. A few moments later Liz heard the clatter of her riding boots on the tiled hall, followed by her tread on the stairs.

'Liz.' Norma's voice was soft, yet strained, from half-way up the staircase. 'I'd like a word with you, please.'

Liz darted across the room and turned the key in the door. She just couldn't face another scene with Norma.

She went back to the bed, sitting on the edge as Norma knocked at the door, and then turned the knob.

'Open this door, please, Liz,' came Norma's voice. 'I know you're there.'

Liz fought to keep her silence. She couldn't trust herself to speak. She was tight-lipped as she stared at the locked door, uncomfortably aware of Norma who was waiting for her on the other side.

Norma rapped again as though she intended to keep on knocking until the door was opened.

'Go away!' Liz called. 'Please go away.'

The knocking stopped.

CHAPTER IV

THAT MYSTERY BOY AGAIN

Liz pressed a hand against her aching head. She could not stay in her room for ever. Sooner or later she would have to face Norma. And then what?

Suppose she saved herself the humiliation of being turned out of Ponyways by packing her suitcase, and leaving of her own free will? But wouldn't that be playing into Norma's hands? What could she do?

She took off her spectacles and put them on the dressing-table. She went to the wash basin, and splashed her face with cold water. She wiped her face dry, blew her nose hard and put on her spectacles.

She turned to the window as she heard the crunch of hooves on gravel, and the voices of Toni, Rosemary and Fay when they came into the house with the shopping. In a moment they would be starting to get the lunch.

Well, there was only one thing for it, Liz decided. She would go downstairs and face Norma.

'I wasn't a coward when I pushed down those jumps,' she told herself, 'so why would I be one now?'

She walked to the door. Her determination weakened as she heard Norma's voice from the hall below: 'Fay, please come here a moment.'

There was the shutting of a door, and muffled voices, mostly Norma's, drowned a moment later by laughter from the kitchen and the clatter of pans, and Toni's voice calling: 'Wanted – three volunteers to peel the potatoes! You, you – and oh, where's Liz?'

Liz went back to the looking-glass, and combed her hair. Now for it. She was about to unlock the door when she heard footsteps on the landing, followed by a light knock.

'Liz!' It was Fay's voice at the door. 'May I come in please?'

Liz felt her heart thudding. What now?

'Just a moment, Fay.'

Liz turned the key. Fay stood in the doorway, her eyes solemn in her kindly young face.

'Norma called me into the study,' Fay said quietly. 'She seemed rather on edge. She asked me to bring you this note. Goodness knows what it's all about, and why she's bothered to write a note when surely she could shout upstairs to you.' She handed Liz a sealed envelope. 'There's something lumpy inside it. But I suppose I'm being inquisitive. Don't tell me if it's anything private.'

Liz opened the envelope and took out a folded sheet of writing-paper. Was this what she dreaded, a note to tell her to pack and go? But no, there was something inside the paper. Liz unfolded it and a fox's head tie-pin fell on to the carpet. Liz stared at it, puzzled. She looked at the note.

Dear Liz,

Be a saint and forgive me! You were absolutely right. I was driving Destiny too hard.

Please accept this fox pin as a peace offering.

Yours,

Norma.

'Well!' Liz gasped, picking up the pin. 'If this doesn't beat everything!'

'What's happened?' Fay asked. 'Is anything wrong?'

'No, infant,' Liz gave a happy smile. 'Everything's right. Very right!' She pinned the fox brooch on her tie. 'It seems I misjudged Norma.'

'So you had a row,' deduced Fay. 'And now you've made friends again. I'm so glad. Norma has a lot to live up to being married to a man who is so idolized by us all.'

Liz nodded.

'We'll all have to see what we can do to help,' she told

Fay. 'Lead on.' She moved to the door. 'Quick march to the kitchen. I'll show you how to make an apple Charlotte.'

All through lunch Norma went out of her way to be charming to everybody, and she was especially friendly to Liz.

'I've been thinking that it might do Mike good to see some of you young people,' she announced, smiling round the table. 'So how about you coming with me to the hospital this afternoon? Liz, you must come. He'll particularly want to see you.' She glanced round. 'What about you, Molly? You'll be a soothing influence in the sick-room, I'm sure.'

'Oh, Norma. Thanks!'

Both Liz and Molly were delighted.

After lunch Norma backed out Mike's shooting-brake, and Liz and Molly climbed in.

'Tell Mike to be quick and get better.'

'Give him our love.'

Shouted messages pursued the brake. Then Fay came running down the front steps, plaits flying. Norma pulled up as she caught sight of Fay, in the driving mirror, signalling her to stop.

'Give Mike this, please,' Fay put a little carved horse into Norma's hand, 'for luck!'

Norma smiled, thoroughly pleased.

'Why not give it to him yourself?' she suggested. 'Climb into the back.' She laughed. 'Goodness knows what the hospital will say to so many visitors, but perhaps they'll let us see Mike in relays.'

As the shooting-brake sped down the drive, the others mustered for duty.

'Let's give the house a really good clean through,' suggested Cherry.

'Must we?' Rosemary groaned. 'Oh, very well. I'll wipe down the kitchen paint.'

'Bags I polish the horse brasses,' said Dave.

'And I will polish the sitting-room floor,' said Toni.

'Gerry and I will beat the rugs,' eagerly offered George for both twins. 'We'll use those super rug-beaters that are in the glory-hole.'

'Yes, to crown each other!' Cherry knew the brothers' capacity for mischief when they were doing chores together. 'One of you had better help Toni; then Rosemary can do the rugs.'

'Very well. I'll clean Candy's and Floss's kennels and runs,' volunteered Gerry.

'And I'll saw logs for the sitting-room fire,' Pete decided. 'So that we can have tea round a fire when the others get back.'

By four o'clock everything was ready. Two laden tea trolleys were ready to be pushed into the sitting-room. Then, just as the shooting-brake rolled up the drive, the telephone in the hall rang shrilly. Cherry answered it.

'Cablegram,' Cherry ran to meet the brake. 'It's just been read over the phone, Mrs Dashmore. It's for you.'

'For me?' Norma looked slightly startled. 'What does it say?'

'Mrs Mike Dashmore Ponyways.' Cherry stood on the front steps and read from the slip of paper on which she had copied down the message. 'It was handed in at Nice in the south of France. It says: *"Meet me Radley airport seven p.m. Stay with me overnight at Airport Hotel to discuss my plans."*' She paused. 'It's signed "*Mummy*".'

'How tiresome for Mummy! Her money must have run out.' Norma sighed. 'Well, poppets—' she smiled at them—'you'll be able to carry on without me, I'm sure. Anyway I should be back tomorrow morning.'

'We'll cope,' Liz said readily. 'Don't worry about us.'

'Right then.' Norma was preoccupied. 'I'll just go indoors and pack a bag.'

'You must have some tea before you drive all that way, Mrs Dashmore,' Cherry urged. 'We've got it all ready. You'll have plenty of time.'

'Well, yes. I might just gulp down a cup.'

Toni turned to Fay as they went to push in the tea trolleys.

'How was Mike?'

'Quite cheerful,' Fay reported. 'He looked a bit pale. Otherwise he was just as usual, joking and trying to keep everyone in high spirits, as he always does. Norma says the Sister in his ward told her he'd be home quite soon.'

'Oh, good,' Toni said, relieved. 'By the way, Cherry's organizing a picnic ride this evening.'

After tea Norma set off on the eighty-mile drive to Radley airport, and the children saddled the ponies and rode off, with the dogs, Candy and Floss, running alongside. They galloped along the sands, lit a driftwood fire in the lee of a breakwater, sizzled sausages on sticks and roasted potatoes in the ashes. Then they rode over the headland, while the rippling lane of gold below them turned to red as the sun sank into the sea. Soon they were trotting up the winding tree-lined drive, and there ahead of them was Ponyways.

That night Toni yawned contentedly as she got into bed in the chintzy room under the eaves which she shared with her cousin.

'Sweet dreams of ponies!' she murmured.

'And long live Ponyways!' Rosemary snuggled down between her sheets. 'Say I!'

A full moon, shining through the window into Toni's eyes, almost dazzled her. Something had made her wake up with a start. She listened.

She heard the clatter of hooves on the cobbles of the yard. Quickly she jumped out of bed and ran to the window. She blinked in amazement at the moonlit scene below. A slim boy, with yellow hair, was leading Catkin from the stable. Who was the boy? He was not one of the guests who was staying at Ponyways. Another odd thing was that he was wearing evening dress – white tie and tails, as though he had been to a dance or a party.

What was the stranger intending to do with Catkin? Toni

glanced at her wrist-watch on the dressing-table. The hands pointed to ten past two. She looked across at Rosemary's bed. Her cousin was stirring in her sleep.

Just then Catkin whinnied and Toni stared down at the yard again. The boy had turned his head. He was looking up at her window. Had he seen her watching him? Now the moon shone full on his features. He was an unusually handsome boy, with the bluest of blue eyes, full lips and well-formed features. She had the feeling she had seen him before, perhaps only once. But where, and when?

Suddenly she remembered. He was the boy who had appeared in the back doorway of Ponyways soon after she and Rosemary had arrived there. No one had known him. He had smiled, scarcely said anything, and then walked past them, through the kitchen and into the little room that Mike used as his study. When Pete had gone looking for the strange boy a few moments later, he had completely vanished. No one had seen him or heard anything about him again, and the minor mystery had been forgotten, until now.

Toni noticed that the pony was saddled and bridled. The boy was tucking his trouser legs into his socks, about to mount. Toni put out a hand to open the window, but she drew it back when she heard Rosemary's voice.

'What's going on?' her cousin asked, sleepily, sitting up in bed.

'It's the mystery boy again!' Toni reported in a whisper. 'You remember! That yellow-haired boy who suddenly appeared on the day we arrived – and then just walked out. He's down there, in white tie and tails, making off with Catkin.'

'What! You must be dreaming!' Rosemary exclaimed, jumping out of bed to join her cousin.

Toni flung open the window and both girls craned out.

'Hey, there!' Toni called to the boy who was now in the saddle. 'Who are you? What do you think you're doing?'

The boy looked up at them. He seemed slightly startled, but not for long. A smile lit up his good-looking face.

'I'm borrowing this pony,' he told them. He spoke in a

pleasant, well-bred voice, with the hint of a drawl. 'Sorry I disturbed your beauty sleep. Good night, or should I say good morning?'

'Well, he's a cool customer!' Rosemary exclaimed. 'Hey, come back!' she shouted as the boy calmly walked Catkin out of the yard. 'You can't do that.'

'But I am doing it!' the boy called over his shoulder, and his light-hearted chuckle spurred the two girls to further action while, from the dogs' run, Candy and Floss barked sleepily.

'We must stop him.' Toni pulled on her jodhpurs. 'It may be a joke. I know! He might be someone who knows Mike – someone who has a right to borrow a pony, even at this time of the morning. But we can't risk it, because *he might be stealing Catkin*!'

'He might be doing it for a dare, or a bet,' Rosemary said, snatching up her riding jacket. 'But it seems *crazy*, doesn't it? Imagine anyone going for a moonlit ride in white tie and tails.'

The cousins ran downstairs, and were in too much of a hurry to notice that the hall light was already switched on. When they sped along the first landing, they saw Pete below in the hall, looking as if he, too, had dressed in a hurry. Pete was tugging back the front-door bolts.

'So you saw that boy with Catkin?' Toni gasped.

'Yes,' Pete said quickly. 'I woke up to hear you challenging him. I thought I might have time to creep out and surprise him while you were still talking to him.' He flung open the door, and led the rush down the steps and along the path to the stables at the back of the house. 'Come on. We'll give him a run for his money.'

There was no time to saddle the ponies. Toni took Lochinvar's bridle from the tack-room and hurried to the big horse's loose box. She wanted a reliable mount that could stand the pace.

'Steady!'

She quietened the surprised horse as she slipped on his

bridle and led him out. Lochinvar was sixteen hands, so she had to use the mounting block to reach his bare back. Rosemary was already on Russet, and Pete vaulted easily on to Black Boy. They jostled through the yard gateway, across the paddock and jumped the fence.

Toni's legs gripped Lochinvar's sides as he rose to the

fence. She swung her body forward. The big horse cleared the jump easily. They landed smoothly and cantered along the sandy track that led up to the Downs.

'There he is!' Rosemary exclaimed. 'See him? By the lime trees.'

Ahead, in the bright moonlight, Toni could see the boy and Catkin. He must have heard the beat of the following hooves, because he turned in the saddle and gave his chasers a nonchalant, and encouraging, wave. Then he swung Catkin on to the springy turf of the Downs, and broke into a gallop.

'He doesn't seem to be worried about our following him,' said Toni. 'I wonder why not.'

Sweat broke on Lochinvar's neck as he pounded up to the ridge. Then his nostrils caught the fresh wind that blew from the sea. He tossed his head and galloped eagerly after Catkin whose grey body showed for a moment on the skyline before disappearing into a dip on the Downs.

With Rosemary and game little Russet well behind, Pete urged Black Boy in fast pursuit.

The yellow-haired boy led them into the shadows of a wood, along a path that twisted beneath the stunted, wind-swept trees; then up the steep slope of Beacon Hill. Catkin climbed steadily, but Lochinvar and Black Boy, with their greater weight, were getting blown. Toni and Pete had to dismount and lead them up the last hundred yards of rocky ground.

Toni scrambled up the Beacon Cairn to remount Lochinvar. While the big horse got back his breath, she scanned the moonlit countryside below them.

'There he is,' Pete gave an excited 'Tally Ho!' as he saw Catkin and the yellow-haired boy in the grassy hollow below.

'Now he really is trying to shake us off,' Toni decided, urging Lochinvar down the hillside after the mystery boy.

Lochinvar managed the steep descent and reached the valley in time for Toni to see the yellow-haired boy waiting for them. He had reined-up Catkin, and was motionless on his mount, like some moon-bathed statue.

Toni trotted towards him. He was smiling while he watched her. She slowed Lochinvar to a walk as she heard the hoof-beats of Pete's and Rosemary's ponies coming up behind.

'Come on!' the boy called challengingly. 'Don't be scared of me!'

CHAPTER V

ADVENTURE BY MOONLIGHT

'It would take more than you to frighten me,' Toni retorted, riding towards the yellow-haired boy.

He waited until she was within six yards of him. Then he turncd Catkin to canter towards the chalky ridge behind an old quarry.

Toni reined-up by a lightning-stricken oak tree. When the boy realized that she was no longer following him, he slowed Catkin to a walk, and looked back at her as if daring her to take up the chase again.

At that moment Pete cantered up to Toni.

'There he is,' said Toni. 'Up above the quarry. I think he's playing some kind of game with us. I've a good mind to give up and go home.'

'And let him get away with Catkin?' Pete protested. 'No fear! Catkin's a valuable pony, and we can't have practical jokers borrowing Mike's ponies at all hours. We've got to catch him. Come on.'

Pete set Black Boy up the path that led to the top of the quarry.

Chalk dust blew into Toni's eyes and throat as Lochinvar followed Black Boy's scrambling hooves.

'Where's he making for now?' she groaned as they galloped over the short turf to Saddle Ridge.

'He's leading us in a circle!' Pete sounded determined. 'But we'll catch him yet.'

Toni saved her breath. She was too busy keeping her wits alert as she cantered Lochinvar downhill, avoiding the old rabbit burrows that pitted the ground.

'Now what is he doing?' Pete was baffled as he pulled up at the Sheep Dip and saw the boy turn Catkin down the sandy track that led back to Ponyways. 'Well, I'm dashed! He's taking us home.'

'I think that's what he meant to do all along,' Toni sighed. 'He's just out for a moonlit joy-ride.'

'We'll catch him when he gets to Ponyways,' Pete declared angrily, urging Black Boy to give his last ounce of speed. 'I'm going to find out what he's up to!'

Even the gallant Catkin was flagging now, and the stamina of the two bigger horses was beginning to fail. Toni saw the distance between them shorten as they galloped after the boy down the track.

'Come on, Lochinvar!' She leaned forward to whisper into her mount's ear. 'We've nearly caught him.'

Just ahead Catkin rallied herself to a last effort as she approached the paddock fence. She was only a fourteen-two pony, and the fence was four feet six. Her front legs caught it sharply and she came down. The yellow-haired boy somersaulted over her head and lay on the grass in the paddock.

Toni reined-up Lochinvar, dismounted and tied him to the fence as she hurried to the rescue.

Catkin was already scrambling up. Her martingale strap dangled, broken, between her legs. She was winded and her flanks were heaving while she stood near the boy who lay quite still.

'I say!' Pete jumped down from Black Boy and scrambled over the fence to join Toni. 'This fellow's had a nasty fall.'

'He's unconscious,' Toni gasped, bending over the boy. 'Is – is he badly hurt, do you think, Pete?'

Pete gently turned the boy over on to his back. The boy's arms fell limp at his side. In the moonlight Pete saw a bruise on his forehead near a hank of yellow hair which had fallen over his brow.

'I think he's just knocked out,' he reassured Toni. 'We'd better get him into the house.'

'Goodness!' Rosemary pounded up on Russet and came over the fence to join them. 'What's happened? I thought I'd never get here. Russet just couldn't keep up. Let me help.'

'You two girls take his legs,' Pete directed. 'I'll take his shoulders, and we'll carry him into the house.'

Meanwhile Candy and Floss were jumping up at the wire-netting of their run, barking wildly, and trying to see what was happening. Wakened by the noise, most of the other young guests thronged the hall.

'What's been going on?' Liz was tying the sash of her dressing-gown as she came downstairs.

Briefly Pete explained.

'We'll put him on the spare divan in Mike's study,' Liz decided. 'Who is he? Does anybody know?'

Everyone looked blank.

'Perhaps we ought to go through his pockets, and see if there are any papers, or letters or anything that will give us a clue,' suggested Dave.

'It wouldn't really be prying,' said Cherry, 'because this is an emergency.'

Pete gently felt in the boy's pockets and brought out some loose change and coppers, and a torn piece of paste-board.

'Hullo! What's this?'

'The return half of a railway ticket from Drayfield to Dunmouth,' Liz said. 'Now let me see, Drayfield's about three miles away. There was a dance at the County Hotel there last night, and Dunmouth's about twelve miles across the Downs. Perhaps he'd missed the last train, and was borrowing a pony to go home.'

'He may be a friend of Mike's,' said Gerry.

'Or of Norma's,' put in George.

'Anyway he's someone who knows his way around Ponyways,' said Rosemary. 'Remember how he walked in as though he owned the place, and then walked out again a week or so ago?'

'He's coming round!' said Liz. Being the eldest, and a doctor's daughter, she felt she should take charge. 'Leave this to me.'

The boy's eyes flickered open. He gazed up at them all in a puzzled way.

'I took a toss, didn't I?' He sat up and gingerly felt himself. 'Well, there don't seem to be any bones broken.'

'We were just going to call a doctor,' said Liz.

'I don't need one.' He lay back on the pillow and gave a tired sigh. 'Buzz off, everyone. Put off the light, and leave me in peace.'

'That's all very well,' Pete began, 'but there are one or two questions we'd like answering.'

'Not now!' the boy murmured. 'Leave it until morning ... Good night.'

Liz bent over him. 'He's asleep, or pretending to be.' She turned to the others. 'We'll have to leave our curiosity unsatisfied until breakfast-time.' She ushered everyone into the hall, clicked off the study light, and quietly shut the door. 'Rub down the ponies, and get back to bed everyone.' She glanced at the hall clock. 'Goodness! It's twenty-five past three.'

Next morning everybody seemed to oversleep. It was half past nine when Toni opened her eyes to hear the dogs barking to be let out.

'Hurry up, Rosemary,' she told her cousin, picking up her towel and sponge-bag before going to the bath-room to wash. 'We're going to be dreadfully late, and Norma's coming back this morning.'

A quarter of an hour later Toni went downstairs to find Liz in the kitchen, putting on the kettle.

'How's the mystery boy?' she asked.

'Still sleeping,' Liz said, reaching for the sliced bread and stacking it on two large plates. 'I'm going to waken him as soon as I've made the tea. Then we'll find out who he is.'

She broke off as she heard a vehicle coming up the drive.

Toni ran to the hall to look out of a window.

'It's Norma!' she announced. 'And she's got her mother with her.'

'You're just in time for breakfast,' Liz welcomed the mother and daughter as they walked into the hall.

'I'm afraid we're very late this morning,' Toni apologized.

Mrs Gill gave a noncommittal smile. She was a willowly fifty with smoothly-coiled flaxen hair and a figure-hugging black suit. 'I never take breakfast,' she confided to Liz. 'Just hot water with a slice of lemon. But if you've made coffee I could do with a cup now.'

'There's been an accident,' Toni was telling Norma. 'Nothing very serious. Some boy or other borrowed one of the ponies in the small hours. Pete, Rosemary and I chased him, and he had a fall. He was knocked out and we don't know who he is. He's in Mike's study on the divan.'

'Good gracious!' Norma's mother swept up the steps and into the house. 'Midnight steeplechases! What on earth has been going on here?' Her glance swept round the hall. 'No *flowers*? Really, Norma, that alcove is *made* for hydrangeas. I can see I shall have to get you organized.'

Toni's heart sank. She was thinking that Norma's mother did not look at all domesticated. Mrs Gill's efforts would be entirely – and probably bossily – managerial.

'Now where's this boy?' Norma went into the study. 'Good heavens!' She gazed at the sleeping figure on the divan. 'It's Robin!'

'We thought you or Mr Dashmore might know him,' said Liz.

'Know him!' Norma echoed. 'Of course I know him. He's my *brother*!' She shook the sleeping boy. 'Robin! Hey! Wake up!'

'Hullo!' Robin sat up sleepily. 'Where am I? Oh, I remember! My head!' He touched his forehead. 'It does ache.'

'My poor lamb!' Mrs Gill cooed, kneeling by the divan.

'He was only knocked out,' Liz said reassuringly.

'Only knocked out!' Mrs Gill echoed. 'The poor boy! Never mind, darling. Mother's here now.'

Robin winced as she put a hand soothingly on his bruised brow.

'Ouch! Let up! My head hurts worse when you touch it!'

Norma looked down at him.

'What happened, Robin?' she asked. 'And why were you borrowing one of our ponies in the small hours?'

'I'd been to the dance at Drayfield,' Robin said. 'I missed the last train back to Dunmouth and couldn't get a lift. It was a lovely moonlit night so I thought I'd ride back. Then these girls —' he looked at Toni, Rosemary and Pete who had just come in '— and that boy chased me. I think they thought I was stealing one of your ponies.'

'If only you'd stopped to explain who you were,' Toni began, but gave up with a sigh as Mrs Gill held up a hand to silence her.

'I don't think we ought to bother Robin just now,' Mrs Gill said. 'Would you all leave us?'

Back in the kitchen, the young guests tried to control their impatience.

'Some mother!' Pete growled. 'I pity the "poor lamb".'

'Now one can see what Norma's had to put up with – a mother like that and a brother like Robin!' said Toni.

'And they're being wished on Mike,' sighed Rosemary. 'What a life!'

Liz looked up from the stove. 'Hand me that tray, Fay. That's it.' She put on it a plate of bread and butter, a boiled egg, and three cups, and a coffee jug. 'You're a willing pony, Fay, so you shall have the pleasure of taking in some sustenance to the clan Gill.'

Fay knocked on Mike's study door. Mrs Gill, Norma and Robin were deep in conversation, but they stopped talking when she came in, and it was not until she was out of earshot that they began to speak again.

'Dunmouth's not a bad place,' Robin Gill was telling his mother and sister as he took the top off the boiled egg, 'but it's not much fun for a chap to be living in lodgings, particularly when he's kept short of money.'

'I'm sure I send you all I can spare,' Mrs Gill told her son. 'And you earn quite good wages for a boy of seventeen, in that estate-agent's office.'

'Not any more,' sighed Robin. 'I resigned a week ago. I somehow think they were glad to see me go.'

'Oh, Robin!' Norma put in. 'And you had such good prospects!'

'I might have been in the big money by the time I was forty, grey-haired and quite ancient,' Robin retorted, and sulkily began to eat his breakfast.

'Well, we'll try to fix you up with another job in Dunmouth,' said Norma.

Robin shrugged. 'There's no hurry. Anyway, there's no point in going back to my old lodgings, except to collect my gear. The landlady won't have me back again. I'm not exactly the star-boarder type, you know. Among other things, Mrs Briggs doesn't like my guitar.'

'Your what?' asked Norma.

'My guitar,' Robin explained, patiently. 'I'm buying it by instalments, on hire-purchase.' He took a drink of coffee. 'Mrs Briggs doesn't seem to care for rock 'n' roll.'

'Really, Robin, you're impossible!' Norma sighed. 'What are we going to do with you?'

Robin sprawled on a pile of cushions.

'Well, since the Mater's staying here until her next quarter's allowance comes through,' he added, with a charming smile at his mother, 'I think it's no more than a son's duty to be by her side.'

'Robin's right!' decided Mrs Gill. 'For the time being we'll stay with you, Norma dear.'

Norma looked worried.

'We're rather full up,' she said, getting up to consult the list of bookings, drawing-pinned to the wall above Mike's desk. 'But maybe we could manage it.'

'Of course you can,' Mrs Gill said almost snappily. 'You run a guest-house. And yet you quibble about making room for your own flesh and blood!'

'I'm not quibbling,' Norma said patiently. 'I'm trying to think of ways and means.'

'Mrs Dashmore!'

Norma went to the study door as she heard Fay call from the hall.

'Telephone,' Fay told her. 'It's the almoner of the Drayfield Hospital.'

Norma anxiously spoke into the telephone.

'Mrs Dashmore here ... Yes, I understand ... Very well. Thank you. Good-bye.'

She put down the telephone and turned to everybody within sight. 'It's good news! Mike's being brought home this morning by ambulance.'

'Oh, super!' exclaimed Dave.

'And my mother and Robin are staying with us for a while.' She paused, but there were no exclamations of pleasure at this news. 'So we'll have to see how we can squeeze everybody in. We're going to have rather a full house. Liz, dear, come with me and we'll see if we can put up camp-beds in some of the bigger rooms, so as to free a bed for Mummy.'

Norma and Liz had barely gone out of sight, up the stairs, when Fay noticed, through the glass panel of the front door, three figures on the top step. The bell pealed, and Rosemary opened the door. Standing there, suitcases in their hands, were a tousle-haired boy in tweed hacking-jacket and grey corduroy trousers, and two girls in duffel coats.

'Hullo, everybody!' The elder of the two girls, a jolly-looking fourteen-year-old, with tawny hair and a freckled nose, led the way into the hall. She looked round with pleasure. 'It doesn't seem a year since we were here last. Oh, it's lovely to be back again. And where's Mike?'

'My son-in-law's in hospital,' Mrs Gill told them as she came out of the study. 'And Ponyways is already full up.'

'But it can't be.' The boy came forward. 'We booked up months ago. I'm Philip Forester and these are my sisters, Sheila and Jane. Aren't you expecting us?'

'Well, I certainly wasn't,' Mrs Gill said firmly. 'And I'm very sorry, but there simply isn't any more room. There must be some muddle, a double booking or something like that. You'll have to go home.'

'But we can't. We haven't a home to go to. It's all shut up,' Jane pointed out. 'Mummy and Daddy have left for Italy on their own holiday. They'll be in the air by now.'

'This is dreadful!' Mrs Gill put a hand to her head. 'This house will be a bear-garden, and I do need rest after that dreary journey from Nice. And my son and son-in-law *must* have quiet after their injuries. I'll have to make other arrangements for you all.'

Nonplussed, they gazed at her as she picked up the hall telephone. What was she going to do now?

'Hullo.' The children heard her speaking to the operator. 'Give me the biggest local hotel ... Hullo,' she said again, a few seconds later. 'Is that the manager of the Cove View? This is Mrs Mortimer Gill. I'm speaking from Ponyways. Can you give me some sort of accommodation for a number of children, mostly teenagers. About a dozen ... Well, haven't you an annexe? The other hotels will be full, too! Well, what happens in an emergency? I mean there must be some sort of accommodation for refugees, or flood victims ... Who? ... Oh, yes, I see. Thank you *so* much ... You're most helpful.'

Toni, Rosemary and Pete looked at each other in dismay as she rang off. Would she really turn them all out of Ponyways in the middle of their holiday there?

Mrs Gill was telephoning again. 'Is that Mrs Johnson? I understand you're on the Village Hall Committee. Good. Well, this is Mrs Mortimer Gill from Ponyways. There's been an emergency and I want to accommodate some people in the Village Hall. I understand you have the keys. There are camp-beds, I take it, and blankets? Oh, there's a field-kitchen, too. Excellent. No, not refugees – well, perhaps in a way – yes, *quite* a disaster – but you must let them sleep there. There's nowhere else for them to go. I assure you it is an emergency. There's *illness* in the house. *Two* accidents. Absolute quiet is essential. Thank you so much. I shall be most grateful. I'll tell them to come for the keys on their way.'

She put down the telephone and turned to the children.

'Well, that's all arranged,' she told them. 'You'll be able to camp out in the Village Hall. There's a field-kitchen there. You'll find it great fun. I want you to pack your things as quickly as you can and move out right away. There are two big rooms, apparently, one for the boys and one for the girls, and there's a kitchen, some quite comfortable beds and plenty of bedding. You'll have a splendid time.'

'But what about our riding holiday?' Toni asked. 'And what about the ponies and horses? There won't be anybody to look after them.'

'You'll come back here, of course, between meals.' Mrs Gill thought quickly. All those animals must need a great deal of looking after. 'Now, hurry up and pack.'

'Well, I like that!' murmured Toni, as they went upstairs to their rooms, 'Mrs Gill's even more impossible than Norma.'

'Sssh!' warned Rosemary. 'Here she is.'

'Oh, Norma,' Toni said quickly, seeing Norma and Liz edging out of the box-room carrying a camp-bed between them. 'We're just going to pack. Mrs Gill's moving us into the Village Hall.'

'What!' Norma gasped. 'Gracious me! Wait a minute, please.'

She hurried downstairs. They heard her go into the study and shut the door.

'Now who'll win, Norma or her formidable Mama?' Toni speculated, sitting on the top stair.

'Do you realize what you've done, Mother?' Norma was protesting. 'These children are *paying guests*. Besides they're so useful.'

'Children can't do as much as all *that*, Norma dear,' Mrs Gill said smoothly. 'And this place really is a madhouse. Hordes of adolescents everywhere, mostly covered in straw and smelling of stables! It's impossible!'

'Not half as impossible as it will be without them,' Norma pointed out. 'We haven't any servants, you know. These children have been doing the cooking and the washing-up. They've even cleaned through, as a surprise. Don't you understand, Mother? We can't run the house without them.'

'There simply isn't room for them all to sleep here,' Mrs Gill said. 'I must have a room to myself and so must Robin. You and Mike have your own room, of course. And now there are these three extra children! Besides I've already made other arrangements for them.'

'Now, look here, Mother,' Norma protested. 'You've been here only ten minutes, and you've started interfering. You've absolutely no right to walk in Mike's house and —'

'Oh, stow it, Norm!' Robin groaned from the divan. 'My head!'

'You see!' Mrs Gill turned triumphantly to her daughter. 'Robin can't stand all these people about, and Mike won't be able to either. Be reasonable, my dear. The children will simply love camping in the Village Hall.'

'Very well,' Norma relented. 'But you'll have to explain to Mike that it was your idea.' She walked to the door. 'So that we have at least some help in the house, I'm going to ask two or three of the most useful children to stay on here.'

'I approve of that,' Mrs Gill nodded decidedly.

CHAPTER VI

YET MORE PONIES

'Poor Fay and Molly – and poor, poor Pete! I'm glad Norma and her mother didn't decide we should be the ones to stay behind at Ponyways,' Toni confided to Rosemary as they helped Liz to pack up some food supplies from the pantry. 'I say, how about a tin of ham?' she added. 'And some tins of sausages and baked beans?'

'Pile 'em in!' approved Dave. 'We'll need plenty of nourishment to make up for the fact that we're being turned out of Ponyways.'

'Of course, it's the absolute limit,' said Liz, bringing some empty cartons from the top of the cellar steps. 'We've all looked forward so much to the day when Mike would come home from hospital, and now that the day's arrived, we're being sent out of the way.'

'I'm sorry for Mike,' Rosemary said, taking a jar of chutney from one of the shelves. 'He's certainly picked a difficult sort of mother-in-law.'

Half an hour later, taking it in turns to push the stable handcart on which their luggage was piled, the Ponyways exiles made their way to the Village Hall.

'Of all the rotten luck!' Cherry groaned as a cream-coloured vehicle came into sight. 'Here's the ambulance with Mike. We'll have missed him by a quarter of an hour.'

'Never mind,' Rosemary said comfortingly. 'We might see him tomorrow when we go to help with the ponies.' She broke off as two big horse-boxes lumbered past them. 'Hullo! I wonder where they're going.'

'Most likely to Ponyways,' said Liz.

'J. Fitt. Horse Dealer.' Cherry read the lettering painted on the back of the last vehicle. 'More ponies! Odd that Norma didn't say anything about them.'

'When ponies are involved,' confessed Toni, 'my curiosity is insatiable. I'll telephone Fay later and find out all about it.'

After they had stacked their kit-bags and suitcases in the Village Hall, Cherry organized the boys into setting up the camp-beds and sharing round the blankets. Liz and Jane and Sheila Forester began to get the lunch.

'Sliced ham and potato salad,' Liz declared, wielding the tin-opener. 'I hope nobody minds.'

'It will be delicious,' said Toni. She helped to put up the trestle tables and carried crockery from the cupboard in the Village Hall kitchen. 'Can you manage now?' She turned to Liz. 'We'll be back in two minutes.'

Toni and Rosemary squeezed into the telephone box at the end of the street. Soon Toni heard Mrs Gill's voice at the other end say sharply:

'Ponyways here. Mrs Gill speaking.'

'Hullo, Mrs Gill,' Toni said after pressing Button A. 'May I speak to Fay?'

'And who is Fay?' Mrs Gill asked in an abstracted way.

'Our friend. She's helping you with the cooking,' Toni explained.

'Oh, the willing child with plaits,' Mrs Gill said. 'Is it important? Fay's so busy. She's peeling the potatoes, and lunch will be late as it is. Ah well, hold on, but please don't keep her for long.'

A few minutes later Toni heard Fay's hullo.

'Fay! What's going on?' Toni asked breathlessly. 'Have two horse-boxes just arrived?'

'Yes, they have.'

'What was in them?' Toni wanted to know.

'Six unbroken horses! Norma's planning to break and school horses and then sell them,' Fay's voice dropped. 'Mike didn't even know they were coming.'

'Gosh! What did he say?'

'I wish I knew.' Fay broke off. 'I'll have to go now. 'Bye.'

At the Village Hall the Ponyways exiles ate their lunch

hurriedly. They were all longing to get back to Ponyways to see the new horses.

As they entered the drive a little later, the Ponyways shooting-brake came out and turned into the main road. Norma was driving and Mrs Gill sat beside her.

'We're off shopping,' Norma called briefly. 'We can't stop now.'

Dave chuckled as soon as they were out of earshot.

'Good! They're having to get more food because we nearly emptied the pantry.' He broke off to listen. 'What's that?'

They heard several notes which sounded as though they were blown on a small brass instrument.

'It's a hunting-horn!' exclaimed Rosemary.

'Mike seems in good spirits,' Liz remarked. 'Perhaps he's sounding the "gone away" because Mrs Gill's gone off for the afternoon.'

'Listen!' said Toni as she heard a series of tootles from the hunting-horn. 'Mike can't be blowing that. It's more like rock 'n' roll than a hunting call.'

'The horses are excited about it,' Liz said as Black Boy, Lochinvar and Catkin cantered to the fence and sniffed the wind, listening for further hunting calls. 'Look out!' Liz sprang forward when six three-year-olds, with coats in varying shades of brown, came thundering across the field after them. 'Try to drive them back.'

The leading horse gave an excited squeal and cleared the hedge. Three of the others jumped after him. Liz and Philip ran to head them back, but the horses dodged them, snorting, and galloped away down the drive.

The remaining two three-year-olds looked undecidedly after their companions. Then, as Toni, Rosemary and Dave ran towards them, waving their arms, they changed their minds and cantered to the far corner of the field.

'Somebody give me a hand,' Cherry urged, dragging the broken-off branch of a tree towards the thin part of the hedge where the horses had broken out. 'We must make up this gap to stop the rest of them escaping.'

The three Foresters ran to help her.

'Come on!' Liz turned to Toni, Rosemary and Dave. 'We've got to act quickly.'

They grabbed saddles and bridles, and halters with which to lead the runaways when they were caught. Then they took the ponies that were nearest the tack-room. These happened to be the polo-ponies, Silver, Barney, Pedro and Juanita. Toni, who always liked a grey, found, to her delight, that Silver nuzzled up to her. She put on his saddle, led him into the yard, and mounted. Next moment Liz came out with Barney.

As they trotted off down the drive, the twins, George and Gerry, panted up.

'Get a couple of ponies,' Liz told them, 'and follow us.'

Rosemary and Dave caught up as Liz and Toni stopped at the drive-end, looking up and down the road.

'There they are!' Dave pointed towards the village.

Toni saw two of the horses eating grass by the roadside.

She put Silver on to the verge and cantered after them.

'Steady!' warned Liz.

Liz's warning came too late. The young horses threw up their heads and cantered off when Silver and Toni rounded the bend.

'That's done it,' Toni groaned, urging Silver to go faster as Liz thundered past on Barney.

The runaways realized they were being followed. Snorting and squealing, they clattered into the village street.

A terrier ran barking from the school caretaker's cottage. The dog nipped the heels of the nearest horse which reared, lashed out and bolted wildly, knocking over the road-sweeper's cart in his fright.

Silver and Barney stopped in their tracks, snorting. They, too, were scared by the clatter of the over-turned hand-cart.

'Oh, Silver! Please be sensible,' Toni coaxed, trying to discourage the polo-pony from waltzing in circles.

Barney would not move. He kept his hooves firmly on the tarmac, and looked down his nose at the road-sweeper's cart. Behind them, Pedro and Juanita showed their carefree South

American temperament by calmly pulling the grass that grew round a chestnut tree near the bus stop. Then they indulged in a lazy siesta while Silver and Barney, still refusing to move, blocked the roadway.

'Why don't you go on?' George panted, cantering up on tubby Samba.

'You're letting them get away!' pointed out Gerry, trying to ride Flinders past the gyrating Silver.

'You're telling us!' Toni managed to calm Silver at last and persuaded him to trot through the village. Barney, following Silver's lead, shied at the roadman's harmless hand-cart.

Toni and Liz reined-up at the cross-roads as Pedro, Juanita, Samba and Flinders trotted up behind.

'Which way now?' puzzled Liz.

'We'd better spread out,' Toni decided. 'Rosemary and I will ride towards the Downs.'

'And I'll take the left fork of the road,' Dave decided.

'We'll go towards the beach.' George spoke for both twins. 'The runaways might have gone that way, or some of them might.'

'Yes, they might have split up,' said Liz. 'Very well, I'll take the Drayfield road.'

As the others rode off in their different directions, Liz put Barney on to the grass verge.

A relentless hot sun now blazed in a cloudless sky. Liz felt dusty and sticky, but she pressed on, driven by anxiety. She reached the main road and felt even more anxious. Anything might happen to four frightened horses on the busy roads among the holiday traffic. Even Barney kept shying and trying to climb up the hedge-bank as cars, charabancs and motor bicycles whizzed past, the drivers intent on quickly getting to the sea.

'Are you lookin' for some boltin' 'orses, Miss?' a farm-hand shouted above the roar of his tractor as he turned into a gateway.

Liz tried to calm Barney who was crab-walking away from the tractor.

'Have you seen them?' she asked, managing to coax the pony into the gateway.

'Aye! Four of 'em went off down yon lane fifty yards back,' the farm-hand shouted.

'Thanks a lot.'

Glad that the runaways had not split up after all, Liz patted the sweating Barney, turned him and rode back along the main road and down the lane that the farm-hand had indicated. Her spirits rose. Ahead she saw the runaway horses, grazing on the grass rectangle near a hedge and a wide driveway.

She slowed Barney to a walk, keeping on the far-side of the lane and trying to skirt round the grazing horses and so catch them unawares.

Suddenly, round the bend towards her, chugged a diesel-roller. Barney took one look at it and reared in fright. The runaways saw the diesel-roller, and galloped through the gateway, past the lodge and up the drive.

Liz kept her seat with difficulty while Barney waltzed round on his hind legs until the diesel-roller had passed them. Then he came down to earth and stood, trembling. Liz stroked his neck to calm him before she cantered him up the drive after the runaways.

She rounded a clump of snow-white, late-flowering rhododendrons in a full-scented bloom, and came within sight of a Regency house. Green shutters were hooked back from the windows and a riot of clematis and scarlet trumpet-creeper flamed against the white walls. But where were the horses?

Across the far lawn strolled a portly figure, resplendent in a light grey check suit, and canary-coloured waistcoat. He had dark hair, and a bristling moustache.

Liz groaned as she recognized him as Winton Blare, television's crustiest panel-game personality. She felt his surprised and disapproving gaze fix on her and Barney. How she wished that Winton Blare were cosily and entertainingly inside a cathode-ray tube, smaller than life and muted to black-and-white. Instead here he was – Winton Blare, very much in person, striding across the lawn towards her. In real life he was even portlier, larger and more angry-looking than when he was reduced to an image on a 17-inch screen. Liz sat astride Barney, longing to reach out, turn a knob and see Winton Blare diminish and disappear. Anyway, what was he doing here? Why wasn't he in the television studios, sponsoring dyspepsia tablets, or rehearsing for the next panel show?

CHAPTER VII

CINDERELLA LIZ

Liz gave Winton Blare a nervously-apologetic smile as he came nearer, and was surprised when he returned it with cordiality.

'Ah, good afternoon, young lady!' boomed Mr Blare.

At that moment a wheelbarrow, pushed by a grey-haired gardener, trundled from behind a yew hedge. Barney whinnied. He was nearly as alarmed by the wheelbarrow as he had been by the hand-cart, tractor and diesel-roller. He backed into a clump of hollyhocks in the herbaceous border. He felt the tickle of *Artemisia lactiflora* against his hocks and lashed out, tipping Liz over his head so that she rolled against the gardener's barrow, and sprawled among its spilled contents – prickly berberis prunings.

'I'm so sorry,' Liz gasped. She gazed up at Winton Blare through her spectacles. 'I'm sure you're going to be angry, and I don't blame you.'

'My dear young lady, I'm not in the least angry.' Mr Blare's tone was deceptively mellow and courtly as he helped Liz to her feet. His eyes were twinkling and he was radiating charm and geniality. 'In fact, I couldn't be more delighted that you have literally dropped in.'

Liz smiled nervously. Was not this other mood of his more foreboding than his anger? Hadn't she seen his victims on the television lulled into serene unguardedness by the Blare charm – only to be completely deflated next moment by the blast of the Blare rage.

'You can be very kind,' she deliberately reminded him.

'I'm delighted to be of service to you.' He gallantly helped to pick bits of berberis from Liz's jacket. 'And I do hope you're not hurt.'

'Only a bit bruised.'

'Hi, there!'

Liz turned to see Winton Blare's famous wife, the clever American actress, Sadie O'Neil, emerge from behind a cedar tree. Sadie was wearing a candy-striped blouse and scarlet slacks. Her Titian-hair and creamy complexion looked even more glamorous in real life than on the television screen.

'Land sakes!' she exclaimed, staring at Liz. 'What goes on?'

'It seems, my dear,' Winton Blare said to his wife, putting a comforting hand on Liz's shoulders, 'that this resourceful young lady was trying to capture the horses which galloped up our drive, and across our lawn only a few moments ago.'

'Well, what do you know?' Sadie turned to smile at Liz with genuine admiration. 'A round-up, huh?'

'I'm sorry about the damage to your lawn, and your flower bed,' Liz apologized. She anxiously looked round. 'Which way did the horses go?'

'Ah, you need not concern yourself on that account,' said Mr Blare. 'I'm not a horsey-man, mind you. In fact I am inclined to agree with that wit who said: "The horse is uncomfortable in the middle and unsafe at both ends." Nevertheless when the runaway horses came into my grounds I tried to act with presence of mind. I realized they were scared so I hurried to fling open the door of our stable. The horses went straight inside. I've told my chauffeur, Hopkins, to get them some straw or whatever it is horses have. Now I suggest that Fielding here —' He beckoned the elderly gardener, 'takes this animal to join them.'

'Yes, sir,' the gardener said, taking Barney's bridle. He turned to Liz. 'He'll be all right with me, miss. I'm used to horses. I was a groom in the old days.'

'Thank you,' Liz said. 'But I've got to take the runaways back to Ponyways.'

'Ponyways!' echoed Winton Blare. 'Isn't that Mike Dashmore's place over the Downs?'

'Yes, do you know Mike?' Liz asked.

'No, but I'd heard that he was a neighbour of ours. Now look, young lady.' He took Liz's arm. 'You can't possibly take those horses back yourself. I'll telephone Dashmore right away, and we'll make some other arrangements to get them back.'

'Yes, and meantime you must come into the house for a long, cool drink,' Sadie invited, 'just as soon as you've satisfied yourself that all the livestock is safe and snug in our stable.'

Liz followed the gardener into the stable. The runaways were calm now, repentant, and ready to behave themselves. Barney seemed quite happy to join the others after his hectic ride.

Liz left Fielding to make much of them, and went back to

the house. As she reached the front Sadie O'Neil came through the doorway to meet her.

'Everything's fixed, honey,' she said. 'I talked with Mr Dashmore on the telephone. He's sending out somebody to round up the rest of the search party.'

'Oh, good!'

'Then I phoned a neighbour who has got a horse-box. He's bringing it over tomorrow to take the broncs back to Pony-ways.' She took Liz's arm, and led her into the hall. 'Oh, and by the way, you're to stay here for the night. Now don't look surprised. Mr Dashmore said it was O.K. by him. We'll need you here to supervise the loading up of those animals to-morrow.'

'I don't know how to thank you.'

'Then don't try.' She gestured to a tray of iced fruit drinks. 'Help yourself.'

Later Sadie led Liz up the wide, crimson-carpeted stairs to a spacious bedroom with damask-curtained windows that led on to a balcony.

She opened a door off the bedroom and turned a knob in the pink-tiled bath-room. Liz watched fascinated as water frothed from the mouths of dolphins into the sunken, shell-shaped bath.

'Now you soak in there and relax,' said Sadie. 'Meantime I'll look out a dress for you. It's lucky we're about the same size.'

Liz felt like pinching herself. Was she dreaming? All this luxury certainly was a contrast to camping out in the Village Hall. How lovely a bath would be after that hot and sticky ride.

'Help yourself to any of those bath essences,' said Sadie, waving a hand towards a shelf of cut-glass bottles. 'And here!' She went to a cupboard and took out a kingfisher-blue bath-robe. 'Lie down and rest when you've had your bath, and then I'll be along with that dress. I've got just the thing for you.'

Three-quarters of an hour later Liz paraded in front of the

looking-glass wearing a dress of frothy white tulle, with a wide pink sash.

'That's terrific,' Sadie, now *soignée* in gold lamé, encouraged as Liz smoothed down the layers of tulle. 'Just the dress for a pretty young girl like you.'

Liz smiled and her own face reflected back at her mistily. Was she actually looking pretty? She could not see very well because she had decided not to wear her spectacles just for that evening.

'Now you need some flowers,' Sadie decided. 'Creamy-pink roses.' She rang a bell. 'Myrtle,' she said to the maid who came in a few moments later. 'Find Fielding and ask him to cut three of those special roses of his. What do they call them? Coy Colleen! Shades of my Irish forebears! Imagine my forgetting.'

'Very good, madam,' the maid said with respectful politeness. 'I presume you wish me to wire the roses into a corsage for the young lady.'

'You presume darned right, honey!' Sadie breezily said to the departing maid. She turned to Liz again. 'Now let's see what we can do about that hair of yours.'

Sadie led Liz to the quilted stool in front of the satin-draped dressing-table. She brushed out Liz's hair to its shoulder-length, holding it this way and that, critically judging the effect.

'That's it,' she announced triumphantly. 'Pony tail, but with something more ritzy than a ribbon.' She picked up the jewel case she had brought with her and took out a sparkling clasp, fixing it in position before handing Liz a silver-backed looking-glass. 'Swell, huh?'

'I'm sure it looks lovely,' Liz said, blinking short-sightedly. She fingered the clasp. 'But I'd be terrified of losing it. These diamonds must be worth hundreds of pounds.'

'They're not genuine,' Sadie explained. She dived a hand into the box and brought out bracelets, necklaces, and ear-rings. 'All paste – theatrical props – gimmicks for the T.V. panel games,' she confided. 'Here!' She held a necklace against

Liz. 'How about this? And this bracelet?' She stood back and admired the effect. 'You look like a million dollars,' she declared. 'Not a cent less!'

The maid brought the corsage of roses which Sadie carefully pinned on the dress.

'There!' Sadie patted Liz on the shoulder before turning to the maid. 'How does she look, Myrtle?'

'A picture!' the maid said with obvious sincerity.

'Come on.' Sadie walked to the door. 'Time for your entrance.' She glanced through the staircase window as a big, black saloon car drew up outside. 'The curtain's going up. The guests are arriving. Oh, didn't I tell you? I'm throwing a party.'

The spacious drawing-room downstairs was soon full of people.

'Ronnie, I want you to know my friend, Liz.' Sadie led her to a fair-haired boy of about sixteen. 'Liz, this is Ronnie Garnett.' Two other youths came across the room towards them. 'Nigel, Sonny, meet Liz.'

Somehow, now that she was bejewelled and glamorized, Liz felt a new confidence. Her other self, bespectacled and bejeaned, would have been clumsy, awkward, adolescent among all these gay strangers. But she had thrown off her inhibitions with her dusty clothes. Now was her chance to sparkle, to be witty, *wanted*.

Ronnie Garnett, the boy film-star, and Nigel Holmes, the junior tennis champion, argued as to who should take her in to dinner, and finally both of them escorted her.

After iced soup, salmon-trout and tender chicken she found herself telling everybody about the exciting chase after the runaway horses.

'And so our gay and charming guest of honour landed far from softly among the prickliest berberis from Fielding's wheelbarrow,' capped Winton Blare.

After dinner more guests arrived. There was dancing to a gypsy band on the lawn amid the falling dusk. Later everybody sat on cushions under the ghostly white goblets of a giant magnolia, and listened to Ray Summerfield singing hill-billy melodies. It was fabulous, Liz thought happily. She had never imagined life could be like this. She seemed to be in a different world – a world where everyone was rich or famous, and where one always ate marvellous food, where swimming-pools were a part of every garden and it was always an enchanted summer dusk. What was even more wonderful and so utterly amazing was that everyone liked her, and thought that she, Liz Stratton, was wonderful, too.

All parties must end. Sleepily the guests went to their cars. Sadie put an arm round Liz's shoulders and led her up to bed.

'Sleep well, honey-child,' she said at the door.

Liz went into the oyster-satin bedroom, sipped the warm milk and nibbled the biscuits which the maid had put on the bedside table. Then Liz stood on the balcony, watching the yellow moon reflected in the swimming-pool, and listening to a nightingale in the beech wood.

Next morning, she was woken by Sadie coming into the room, clad ready for a swim, with a towelling wrap round her, and a spare swimsuit over her arm.

'Are you joining us for a swim?' asked Sadie.

'Rather!' agreed Liz.

Winton was already in the pool, swimming ponderously and waffling like a friendly seal.

After the swim Liz dressed herself in shirt and jodhpurs, and joined Sadie and Winton for breakfast on the terrace. A horse-box arrived half an hour later. Liz supervised the loading up of the horses and Barney, and was about to jump in with them when Sadie touched her arm.

'Winton's sending you back in the Rolls,' she said. 'Hopkins is driving it round from the garage now.'

'Thank you for being so kind to a stranger,' Liz told them as she got into the car. 'You're both wonderful people.'

'Just a couple of lucky phonies,' sighed Winton.

'Speak for yourself, Winton!' Sadie told her husband. 'You may have only buffooned in panel games, sweetie, but I've acted in Ibsen. When I played Hedda Gabler on Broadway – wow! – was I dynamite?' She turned and clasped Liz's hand. 'Please come again soon, Liz. You're a real person. We like you a lot.'

CHAPTER VIII

MIKE FINDS OUT

Life as a 'refugee' at the Village Hall was certainly very different from being a guest at Winton and Sadie Blare's elegant home, Liz thought next evening as she helped to tackle a pile of unwashed dishes in the cloak-room sink before starting to cook supper.

Nevertheless, it had been a good 'horsey' day, she mused. First she and Toni had ridden to Drayfield to take some of the ponies to be shod. Afterwards, they'd had a picnic lunch in the orchard at Ponyways. Then Cherry had organized a mounted treasure-hunt, riding over the Downs and into the villages in search of clues. By evening they were all healthily-tired and ready to 'flop'.

'What bliss it would be to sit down to one of Mrs Roylance's special suppers!' Toni sighed as she started to wipe the pile of crockery.

They had left the breakfast dishes and the picnic cups and now there was a lot of washing-up to finish before they could get supper. How different things had been last year when Mike was a bachelor and Mrs Roylance and Maud did the work of Ponyways. So far none of them had even seen Mike since he had come back from hospital. He had been resting indoors, with his leg in plaster.

'Goodness knows what we're going to eat.' Liz looked inside the almost empty store-cupboard. 'We'll have to ask Norma for some money to buy some more provisions tomorrow.'

Suddenly the outer door of the improvised kitchen opened and the large, comfortable form of Mrs Roylance bustled in, followed by Maud. Both were carrying big baskets covered with white cloths.

'Can it be true?' gasped Toni. 'We were wishing we could sit down to one of your super meals, Mrs Roylance.'

'Tut! tut!' Mrs Roylance looked at the dishes in the sink, at the greasy stove and at the tired youngsters. 'It's a shame!' she declared. 'That's what it is.'

'No good will come of it.' Maud shook her head. 'That I'm sure. Riding all day and working like this at night. They'll outgrow their strength, and that's a fact.'

'Now then, ducks.' Mrs Roylance took the tea-cloth from Liz and pushed her through the doorway. 'You go and have a tidy up ... and keep out of my way while I get weaving. You, too,' she told Toni and Rosemary. 'Off with you. Maud and me are going to see to your supper tonight. 'Ere!' She thrust a folded table-cloth into Cherry's hands. 'If you must do something, you can lay the table. Put this cloth on and set out the knives and forks. For once you're going to eat like young ladies and gents, not like waifs as you 'ave been doin' since you've been evacuated here.'

Thankfully Liz and the others surrendered responsibility and went to the other cloak-room to make themselves tidy for supper.

Toni gave a blissful sigh as she flopped on to her army-blanketed bed.

'Goodness,' she yawned, looking up at the varnished rafters. 'I didn't realize that I was so utterly exhausted. Mrs Roylance and Maud are good sorts!'

'Come an' get it!' Mrs Roylance waddled in about half an hour later with a steaming casserole in her hands. Behind came Maud, carrying a big dish of potatoes. 'I've made you one of my specials. Irish stew like you used to enjoy so much last year.' She turned to Toni. 'It was your favourite, Miss Toni.'

'Wonderful!' Toni took off the lid and began to serve the appetizing stew. 'How have you managed it in such a short time, Mrs Roylance?'

'That'd be tellin',' Mrs Roylance said. 'Taste it! ... There!

That's a bit different from all that tinned rubbish you've been 'avin' lately isn't it?'

'You're both angels,' Liz told them.

'Well, Maud and me couldn't stand by an' see you goin' on like you was doin',' Mrs Roylance declared, 'when you're supposed to be 'avin summer 'olidays. So we're goin' to come in 'ere every mornin' to look after you. All you need do is to make your beds and get your breakfast. After that it's up to us. How's that suit you?'

'Fine!' Dave said warmly. 'Fay's cooking wasn't bad at Ponyways, but since we've been here everything's come out of tins. We haven't had anything as good as this since we left home.'

'It's scrumptious,' declared George and Gerry in unison.

'Just you eat it up.' Mrs Roylance nodded. 'I've brought a sponge trifle for afters.' She sank into a chair and watched them eat. 'Well, what's the latest? What's been happening at Ponyways? I've 'eard that Mrs Dashmore's mother's moved in? Is that true?'

'Too true!' Rosemary groaned between mouthfuls. 'And Norma's brother, Robin. That's why we've had to come here. There wasn't any room for us.'

'And Mike needs peace and quiet,' Liz added. 'We understand about that. So really we didn't mind moving out if it was going to help him.'

'A nice bit of peace and quiet I reckon 'e's getting!' Mrs Roylance said doubtfully. ''Er Ma's a proper tartar from all I 'ear. Worse than '*er*!' She broke off to listen. ''Ullo! What's that?'

A car horn sounded outside the Village Hall. Next moment the door opened and a middle-aged woman in a green linen dress walked in and gazed round at everybody.

'Mother!' Rosemary jumped up.

'Aunt Meg!' gasped Toni.

'What on earth are you doing here, Mummy? And where's Daddy?' asked Rosemary.

'He's gone to Brussels on a business trip, darling.' The

newcomer kissed her daughter, and then her niece. 'I was at a loose end so I decided to see how you were getting on.' Her glance took in the barely-furnished Village Hall, the wooden beds, the hard chairs, the uncurtained windows, the rough floor. 'It's a good thing I did,' Mrs Brooke added. 'I went to Ponyways and some child told me you'd moved into the Village Hall. I can't understand it, darling. What's been happening?'

'You've a mother's right to know, m'm!' Mrs Roylance broke in whole-heartedly before either Rosemary or Toni had a chance to say anything. 'It's all the fault of the selfish baggage that Mr Mike suddenly went and married. And Mrs Dashmore's mother, too. Between 'em they've turned these poor children out of Ponyways.' She put her hands on her hips. 'I think me and you ought to have a word together, m'm, while these poor lambs finish the supper that Maud and me have brought them.'

'By all means,' nodded Mrs Brooke, taken aback.

'This way then, m'm,' Mrs Roylance invited, showing her the girl's sleeping quarters. 'Look!' She waddled to one of the beds. 'Army blankets and no sheets! I ask you! Maud and me don't work for Mrs Dashmore no more, otherwise we'd have told her wot we thought of this carry on.'

'Sleeping so many in a room,' Maud said gloomily. 'It's enough to make them go into declines.'

'We're just 'elping, out of the kindness of our 'earts, and not even getting paid for it, m'm,' added Mrs Roylance.

'Well, it certainly seems very strange.' Mrs Brooke turned to look at her daughter and niece who were still eating. 'I'm staying at the Castle Hotel in Drayfield tonight, but I'll be going home tomorrow, and I think you two girls ought to come with me.'

'We can't go; we've hardly seen Mike yet,' Rosemary protested. 'He's broken his leg. That's partly why we can't be at Ponyways. Besides, we're loving it here – even though we are roughing it.'

'And now Mrs Roylance and Maud have come to our rescue,

we shall have plenty of well-cooked food,' Toni told her aunt.

'But they can't be expected to work without wages,' Mrs Brooke pointed out, 'even though Mr Dashmore has had an accident.'

'We don't mind about the money, m'm,' said Mrs Roylance. 'Right's right! That's what I say. I don't need paying to do what's no more than my duty by these children.'

'Yes, and I've got my duty, too, Mrs Roylance,' Mrs Brooke said quietly. 'You can't be expected to carry all the burden.' She walked to the door. 'I think I ought to go back to Ponyways and have a talk with whoever is in charge.'

When Mrs Brooke had gone, a delighted smile spread over Mrs Roylance's plump features.

'Mark my words,' she told everybody. 'That's put the cat among the pigeons, an' no mistake!'

Half an hour later Mrs Brooke stood by the window in the study at Ponyways facing Mike Dashmore who was in his wheel-chair.

'I'm sorry that your wife and Mrs Gill have gone out,' Mrs Brooke was saying, 'because I'd have preferred to raise this matter with them, rather than trouble you after your accident.'

Mike Dashmore gave that attractive grin which had won the hearts of most of the girl-guests at Ponyways, as well as of Mrs Roylance and Maud.

'My leg's in plaster, but the rest of me is sound,' he said lightly. 'I can stand shocks. So please be quite frank, Mrs Brooke. Is it about some of the youngsters having to stay at the Village Hall?'

'Yes. And really, Mr Dashmore, I think it's hardly fair we pay you for them to have a riding holiday, and then to be made to live in such discomfort!'

'But Mrs Brooke,' Mike said quietly, 'there's no question of our taking any money for the children while everything's so disorganized.'

'But why was the Village Hall necessary?' Mrs Brooke asked. 'This is a big house.' She looked round. 'I should have thought there would have been room enough for everybody.'

'Unfortunately,' said Mike, 'there wasn't, and my mother-in-law thought it would be best to book the hall, as a temporary arrangement.'

'It's a pity she isn't here,' Mrs Brooke remarked. 'How she can have sent those children to sleep in that damp hall without proper bedding, no sheets and grimy army blankets – well, it's scandalous! And until today, I understand, there was nobody to cook for them.'

'No sheets!' Mike echoed incredulously. 'No proper catering arrangements! But I thought my wife had organized all that.'

'It's obvious you don't know what's going on,' Mrs Brooke said. 'I don't know what to do for the best. Rosemary and Toni seem happy enough. Last year and the year before you looked after them wonderfully, and their riding improved enormously.' She looked uneasily at Mike. 'I just don't know what to say.'

'Let Rosemary and Toni stay if they want to,' Mike suggested. 'I promise things will be better from now on.' His mouth set grimly. 'As to payment, we'll waive that, of course.'

'Well, it's not so much the money as the children's welfare.'

'I quite understand.'

Mrs Brooke held out her hand to Mike.

'I'm sure you'll put things right, Mr Dashmore.'

As soon as Mrs Brooke had gone Mike propelled the wheelchair to the kitchen where Fay and Pete were just finishing an early supper.

'Fay! Pete!' he called. 'Will you push me to the Village Hall?'

'You bet!' Pete offered with a willing grin.

A moment's misgiving seized Fay. 'What about Mrs Dashmore and Mrs Gill? They asked me to keep them a hot supper.'

'Oh, they'll be able to help themselves,' Mike said vaguely.

'I want to find out what kind of a time the others are having.'

An excited chorus of greeting went up when Pete and Fay triumphantly pushed Mike into the Village Hall twenty minutes later.

'Lawks, sir!' Mrs Roylance exclaimed. 'How's your poor leg?'

'Mike! It's Mike!' the Jollison twins shouted.

'Mrs Roylance!' The stern note in Mike's voice was belied by the twinkle in his eyes. 'I didn't know you were still working for us.'

'In a manner of speaking, I'm not,' said Mrs Roylance. 'But somebody 'ad to come and look after these poor lambs.'

'Are you poor lambs?' Mike's eyebrows raised quizzically as he looked round at the young people whom he had grown to regard with affection since they had all become annual visitors to Ponyways.

'Well, Mike,' Liz said candidly, 'you can see for yourself. It's not exactly "homey", is it?'

'We're all right. Really we are!' Cherry assured him.

'One thing's clear,' said Mike. 'You're all being sporting about it. Stick it for tonight. Tomorrow, there will be a lot of improvements.'

At that moment Maud came out of the kitchen, a pile of clean crockery in her hands. 'Oh dear, Mr Mike!' She looked in consternation at Mike's plastered leg. 'I never thought I'd see this day. Tragic, that's what it is, tragic! You in a wheelchair an' all! An' you so young!'

'Come, come, Maud,' Mike said with a robust laugh. 'It's not as bad as all that.'

'Oh, I don't know, sir. There's no end to what can 'appen once you break a bone. P'raps you'll never ride—no, not even *walk* again.'

'Maud!' Mrs Roylance cut in. 'That's quite enough!'

'Sorry, Em,' Maud said. 'Of course we don't want to alarm Mr Mike, do we? Sick people need to be kept cheerful.'

'Maud, you prophet-of-doom!' Mike said breezily. 'You've made me feel on top of the world. I've always regarded your forebodings as a sure sign of good things to come!' He turned smilingly to Pete and Fay. 'Now then, you two. Back to the stables!'

Mrs Roylance fondly looked down the road as Mr Dashmore was propelled through the cool of the summer evening. 'Aint 'e luvl'y? Always a gent. One of the best. That's our Mister Mike!'

CHAPTER IX

ROBIN REBELS

That summer evening, while Norma and her mother were still out, and Fay and Pete were pushing Mike in the wheel-chair from the Village Hall towards Ponyways, Robin Gill was speaking into the telephone, unburdening his frustrated soul to a boy of his own age.

He lolled against the chimney-piece in Mike's study, a discontented expression on his good-looking face.

He was making a trunk call to London. The pips had already gone twice, but still he prolonged the conversation. Why should he worry about the cost of the call? He did not have to pay the telephone bill. That was Mike's headache.

'The Mater's the absolute end, Charteris,' Robin was confiding to his friend who had also left school last term. 'And the atmosphere here, well, it's too ludicrously horsey and hearty. Apart from that the Mater's on at me all the time. Nag, nag, *nag*. And when it's not nagging, it's worse – a cloying possessiveness that's quite pathological.'

'Parents can be very trying,' drawled the other youth.

'And this horsey crowd,' Robin added, 'needs to be seen to be believed.' He laughed. 'I put them in a spin the other day. I borrowed Mike's hunting-horn, and tooted some rock 'n' roll on it. That made Norma's new horses bolt. There was quite a round-up.'

'Ponyways doesn't seem the sort of place for you, Robin,' said Charteris. 'Why not come to London for a few days, and stay with me at the flat? Mother and Father are still in Majorca, so I'm practically on my own except for Bingo from the upstairs flat who drops in to keep me company.'

Robin impulsively looked at his wrist-watch. 'I say, Charteris. Will it be all right if I come tonight? I could just catch the next train. I'd be at your place around midnight.'

'Suits me,' said the voice at the other end.

Robin jauntily put down the telephone. He ran upstairs, two at a time, to his room and began stuffing clothes into his suitcase.

'Hm!' he murmured, pulling out his wallet and examining the contents – a crumpled pound note which he had borrowed from Norma that morning. That would not even pay for his train ticket. Undismayed, Robin glanced round the room.

On the dressing-table were a silver-backed clothes-brush and a photograph in a silver frame of Mike, as a boy rider, putting a pony over a gymkhana fence. Robin took out the photograph and put the frame into his suitcase along with the clothes-brush and an enamel snuff-box from the chimney-piece.

Now what about ready money? He must not be hard up while he was staying with Charteris in London. He hurried to Mike's study and tried the drawers in the desk. One was locked so he 'coaxed' it open with a paper-knife. Robin put the paper-knife into his jacket pocket, together with a glass Georgian paper-weight that had been lying on the desk. In the drawer was a wad of pound notes. He counted out four. Would that be enough? Probably not. He counted out another three.

Hullo! What was that? He listened. Pete and Fay were joking with Mike as they heaved his wheel-chair over the back door-step.

Silently Robin shut the desk drawer and opened the French window.

Carrying his suitcase he walked briskly across the lawn, between the cedars and through a wicket gate on to the road. He held up his hand to halt a small car that came round the corner.

'Could you possibly give me a lift as far as Drayfield Railway Station?' He smiled charmingly at the puzzled woman at the wheel. 'I've had an urgent call to London, and I must catch the next train. So kind of you!'

*

When Mike discovered that Norma and Mrs Gill had not yet returned he asked Pete and Fay to push him round the stables. Destiny began to whinny as soon as the wheel-chair turned into the yard. By the time he reached the loose boxes all the horses and ponies were whinnying and banging their mangers and stable buckets.

Destiny moved to the door of her loose box. Her head came down and her tongue licked Mike's forehead in solicitude, as though he were a foal which had hurt itself.

'What a fuss, old lady!' Mike felt in his pocket for some of the sugar he always carried. 'There! That's more like it.' He patted her neck as she began to crunch the sugar. 'Destiny looks fit,' he told Pete and Fay. 'Has Mrs Dashmore been exercising her?'

'Yes, every morning, Mike,' said Fay. 'She hasn't missed once.'

'Good,' Mike nodded. 'Now let's have another look at the horses.'

Up and down the long lines of stables and portable loose boxes Mike was wheeled. Every door had to be opened and every occupant got a pat and a tit-bit. At last the sugar was all eaten and Mike had to send Fay to the kitchen for more.

'Mrs Dashmore and her mother are back,' Fay reported, returning with a fresh bag of lump sugar. 'They're getting supper.'

'We'll just see the other ponies,' said Mike. 'And then we'll go in.'

After the inspection they went back to the house.

'But, Mike dear, I was going to show you the ponies to-morrow.' Norma came across and took over the wheel-chair from Pete as it neared the kitchen door. She smoothed Mike's hair. 'You look quite tired.' She turned to Pete and Fay. 'You shouldn't let him overdo it.'

Just then Mrs Gill came in, looking worried.

'Look!' She waved a scribbled piece of writing-paper. 'This was on the tray in the hall.'

'Dear Mother, I have been called to London for a few days.

Will write tomorrow. Robin.' Mike read aloud. He tried to disguise his pleasure. 'Well! Well!'

'You haven't been angry with him, Mike, have you?' Norma asked.

'Something *must* have upset him!' Mrs Gill said before Mike could answer. 'He's such a sensitive boy. He must have been quite *distrait* to leave at this time of the night with no word to me, his own mother.'

'He's written you a note,' Norma pointed out. 'So I don't think there's any real reason to flap.'

'And even Robin's departure has its brighter side,' Mike said at last. 'We'll be able to make good use of his room.' He smiled good-naturedly at his women-folk. 'The Village Hall refugees are coming back here tomorrow.'

'Do you mean to say, Michael —' his mother-in-law gazed at him uncomprehendingly — 'that you're planning to move those dreadful, noisy, *horsey* children back into *this* house?'

'Yes, that's the idea,' Mike said lightly. 'This evening I had a visit from a justifiably irate parent. Don't you realize that these children are *paying* to stay here? If anyone moves out it will have to be us.'

'We couldn't,' Mrs Gill said quickly. 'Those children would wreck the house.'

'I doubt it,' said Mike. 'Well then, let's decide how we can contrive to make enough room. Now suppose you move into the small bedroom on the top floor, Mother. That would leave the large bedroom free. There are three beds in there. Yes we should be able to fit in everybody quite easily, after all!'

'Very well,' Mrs Gill said smoothly. 'If you insist on putting me in the attic I'll do as you say.' She gave a martyred smile. 'But I'm quite sure, Michael, that you're making a great mistake. You're wasting this lovely place, filling it with all these tiresome children.'

'Mummy's so right, Mike,' Norma pointed out. 'I was thinking the same thing. Now if we turned Ponyways into an establishment for breaking-in green horses instead of running it as a glorified, horsified, boarding-house for teenagers, well then we really would be doing something worthwhile.'

'You're welcome to break in your young horses as a side-line, dear,' Mike told his wife. 'But our "horsified boarding-house" as you call it, still goes on. As far as I'm concerned we'll be open for our young guests all this summer, next, and the one after, indefinitely.'

Norma looked long at Mike. Fay, at the other end of the room, was watching her. Was she about to rebel? She had risen from the table and was walking across to Mike's wheel-chair. She bent over him and kissed him on the forehead.

'Just as you say, darling,' she said so softly that Fay scarcely heard.

'Phew!' Pete whispered to Fay as they both wandered out of the back door for a late-night stroll in the dusk. 'Some fire-works! But I think Mike's won this round.'

Next morning Liz and Co. moved back to Ponyways, and Mrs Gill moved up to the attic.

Later, as Norma returned from exercising Destiny, she heard Mike call to her from his study.

'What is it, darling?' she asked, going into the room.

Mike was at his desk, rummaging in a drawer.

'Seven pound notes are missing from this wad,' he told her. 'I wondered if you'd had to use them for housekeeping money while I was in hospital.'

'No, Mike.' Norma shook her head. 'Are you sure you haven't taken the money yourself and forgotten?'

'Quite sure,' Mike declared. 'And the odd thing is that my paper-knife and paper-weight are also missing. I thought you might have moved them.'

'I haven't touched them, Mike,' Norma said definitely. 'Don't worry, darling. I expect they'll turn up, and you might have been mistaken about the money. After all you were away a few days, and you were quite ill, you know.'

Mike looked baffled. 'I'm almost sure I locked this drawer.'

He broke off as Liz burst into the study, with Pete behind her.

'Pete says that there was a silver-backed clothes-brush on his dressing-table before he moved out of that room,' she suddenly announced.

'There was,' Pete nodded, 'and a little fancy box on the chimney-piece. They've both gone.'

'Thanks for telling us, Pete,' Mike said soberly. 'Is anything else missing?'

'I don't think so.' Liz seemed reluctant to commit herself. 'Not really.'

'Not really?' echoed Mike. 'What do you mean by that?'

Liz hesitated. 'Well, the twins said they'd lost some chocolate, and Dave missed his pocket-knife, and Toni's somehow mislaid a tie. It's mustard-colour with a hound pattern.'

Mike looked serious. 'It seems as though we've had a burglary while everyone's been out.' He reached for the study telephone. 'This a matter for the police.'

CHAPTER X

NORMA'S PLAN—

'Just a minute.' Norma put out a hand to stop Mike picking up the telephone. 'There's no need to call the police.' She looked uncertainly from her husband to Liz and Pete, wondering whether she should speak in front of them. 'You're mistaken, Mike. Nothing's been stolen. Oh, I know some things are missing, but Robin must have borrowed them, and I swear you'll get them all back.'

'Golly!' gasped Pete.

'O.K., you two,' Mike said quietly to Liz and Pete. 'Things will be sorted out. Cut along now.'

Norma turned pleadingly to Mike as soon as they were alone. 'Don't be too hard on Robin, Mike.'

Mike stared up at her. 'He's in the habit of *borrowing*, isn't he?'

She nodded. 'I'm sorry, darling. I suppose I ought to have warned you. I hoped that Robin would pull himself together when I married you. He'll pawn the clothes-brush and other oddments, but I'll be able to get them back again. He's sure to save the tickets.'

Mike sighed. 'I'll have to take a firm line with him. You realize that, don't you?'

'Yes, darling. But don't worry Mother about this. She'll only defend him. And that makes him worse. She's spoilt him outrageously.'

She broke off as she heard Mrs Gill's voice from the hall.

'Norma! Mike! I've got some news for you.' Mrs Gill walked into the study, waving a telegram. 'This has just arrived. It's from Robin. '*I have been invited to stay with the clan Charteris in Kegan Square. Love Robin*'. How kind of them! She's the Hon. Mrs by the way. I believe they're charming people, and I know they'll just love Robin. Mr Charteris is so influential. He may be able to find a really good job for the boy. Oh, I'm so relieved.' She smiled at her daughter. 'Norma, dear, if Mike can spare you for a moment, please help me pick some roses for my room.'

Some minutes later, Mrs Gill, carrying a basket half-full of Gloire de Dijon roses, paused half-way down the mossy, brick path between the rose beds.

'I know that you want what is best for Mike, dear,' she told her daughter. 'But so often a man does not know what *is* best for him. Then it is the duty of a good wife to influence him in all the subtle ways she can.'

'What are you getting at, Mother?' Norma demanded, trying to hide her irritation.

'I'm thinking of the future of Ponyways,' Mrs Gill said. 'And I'm sure that your talents and Mike's are wasted unless you give up running a holiday home for pony-mad adolescents.'

Norma sighed.

'Try to convince Mike of that!' she said feelingly.

'Yes, I see your point,' Mrs Gill thought for a moment. 'But wouldn't life be spacious and gay if we could have this lovely house to ourselves? You wouldn't have to scrimp and economize. Why you'd make more money out of breaking-in green horses than you would out of these boarders. You've said so yourself.'

'It's what I'd like to do more than anything,' Norma said wistfully.

'And, think of it, I could live with you all the time, dear. There'd be room for me to have my own sitting-room as well as a bedroom, and Robin could invite those charming Charterises here. And think of the enjoyment you'd have with all the new horses.'

'Yes, it would be wonderful,' Norma agreed. 'Mike and I have hardly had a moment to ourselves since we came back from our honeymoon.'

'Well, he's your husband,' Mrs Gill said, 'and it's his duty to consider your wishes. Besides, what *good* are either of you doing running this place as a pony-holiday establishment? The children are only *playing* at ponies. They've been weaned on escapist pony novels and village gymkhanas. You'll never find an international show-jumper among them. If you really put them through their horse-paces, they wouldn't last the course more than a few days. They'd be glad to go home, and they wouldn't want to come to Ponyways again. Try them – and see for yourself!'

That afternoon Liz, Fay, Toni, Rosemary, Pete and the others were saddling-up the ponies when Norma strode into the stables, well-turned-out as ever in her riding clothes.

'I've been talking things over with Mike,' Norma told them. 'And as he's temporarily out-of-action we've decided that I shall take over the riding instruction. You've already lost a lot of time out of the holiday course, so you'll all have to be prepared for some really hard work. I'm counting on you to do your best.'

Liz smiled. This was splendid news. So Norma really was out to do her best for Ponyways and Mike just as she had promised.

'We'll back you up,' Toni assured Norma.

'That goes for us, as well,' said George Jollison.

'It will seem more like the old days when Mike was able to come riding with us,' said Fay. She turned to Norma. 'I think it's wonderful of you to find time to give us riding coaching when you've so much else to do, what with Mike's leg and schooling Destiny. You're a real sport, Norma.'

Norma smiled bleakly. 'I hope you'll still feel like that about me by the end of the holiday, Fay. I'm warning you. The going will be tough.'

'We like it tough,' Pete said.

'Good.' Norma nodded briskly. 'Hurry up all of you. Finish saddling and we'll make a start.'

When all the ponies were ready Norma inspected them to

make sure that bridles were correctly adjusted and girths were tightened. She checked stirrup leathers and safety catches, and reprimanded Dave for having a dirty head-band to his mount's bridle.

'You'll have to clean extra tack tonight, Dave,' she told him, 'to impress on you the importance of clean saddlery. Dirty leather wears out and becomes unsafe. Nasty accidents have resulted from broken stirrup leathers.'

After she had finished her inspection, Norma mounted. A few minutes later, she was leading them at a steady canter over the Downs.

They rode over the ridge, and Norma turned off along the bed of a dried-up stream, through a wood, over some rails and across a meadow towards a ditch with a hedge beyond.

'Come on, you stragglers.' Norma turned in the saddle to shout to Liz and Pete who were gallantly trying to keep up with her.

Dave was feeling wildly for his stirrups after Blackberry's unseating jump over the rails. George had come off when Samba rapped his legs and stumbled. Gerry had lost his crash cap.

'I say,' Pete panted to Liz as he rode alongside. 'I wonder if Norma thinks we're better riders than we actually are. This is a stiff course for the youngsters.'

'Surely she'll soon slacken the pace,' said Liz.

'We're all right, Liz,' Dave said gamely, at last getting one foot into his stirrup iron as he rioted past on Blackberry.

The pony was in a lather. He was grunting excitedly and frothing as he fought his bit, wanting to be in front. All the ponies were fresh. They had not had a great deal of exercise during the past few days and now the rivalry and galloping had gone to their heads.

'You young ones follow me to that gap,' Liz called, riding diagonally across the field where there was a hole in the hedge, and only a ditch to be jumped.

Toni put Catkin at the spot Norma had chosen. The grey took off in a big leap. She was over easily. Rosemary, Cherry and Pete followed, but the three Foresters were in trouble. After Jane had been thrown over her pony's head, and had rolled, relaxed and unhurt, into the ditch, they decided to follow Liz, Dave and the twins through the gap.

Far up the hillside Norma's white shirt showed against the patchy green of the chalky grass. Close on her heels rode Toni, Rosemary, Cherry and Pete. Where Norma led they would follow, Toni decided grimly. They were determined not to be beaten. Behind them struggled Fay and Molly, and, right back, at the bottom of the hill, Liz was shepherding her straggling flock of the younger ones – the Jollison twins, Dave and the Foresters.

Soon they were pounding along the ridge. Southwards the sea sparkled. The ponies seemed to revive as a breeze ruffled their manes. Now Cherry and Toni, Rosemary and Pete felt quite a match for Norma as she took Destiny down a steep path into a disused quarry. The ponies managed the slope without mishap and trotted along a road for a few yards. Then Norma swung off into a green lane, popped Destiny over a low hedge into a field and, skirting the ripening corn, jumped a fence at the far end. Without even glancing behind to see whether anyone was following, she galloped flat out along the Mile Meadow. On to the Downs again she went and then made a breakneck spurt home to Ponyways.

She had rubbed down Destiny and was walking her round the yard when the first of the other riders straggled up the drive.

'Hullo!' Norma smiled coolly. 'I thought you'd appreciate it if I gave you all a run for your money.'

'Oh yes, we do,' gasped Toni. 'But I'm afraid we got rather spread out. Liz would have been here but she stayed behind to lead the younger ones over an easier route.'

Norma nodded absently and took Destiny to her loose box. 'See that everyone dries down and cools off the ponies, Toni dear. I'm going in to change. We'll only have time to snatch a quick tea. Major Nixon, the local vet, is coming along this evening to talk about the anatomy of the horse.'

'Oh, that's grand!' said Rosemary. 'You are giving us a wonderful pony-time, Mrs Dashmore.'

'Am I?' Norma looked blank for a moment. Then she was thoughtful. 'I'll have to see what I can arrange for tomorrow.'

Next morning Norma banged on the bedroom doors at six o'clock. By a quarter to seven they were all doing limbering-up riding exercises. Then there was breakfast to get and stable work to be done. Most of the morning was spent in riding figures-of-eight in the paddock and jumping down the 'grid' which consisted of a fenced-in lane with two-foot-high poles at intervals of a pony-stride along its length. This had to be jumped without stirrups and reins. Afterwards there was elementary dressage and more jumping, this time without saddles and with folded arms.

Of course Mike had given them similar exercises last year, Toni remembered. But he had carefully picked his pupils and he had allowed them only half an hour's such jumping, and then had led a gentle ride round the lanes. Norma kept them at it all morning until Fay, who was never a daring rider, was almost in tears, and the twins and Dave were dead beat.

'Talk about rough-riding!' Pete groaned. 'This is like an army riding course with Norma as Sergeant-Instructor.'

'She's thorough. I will say that for her!' Cherry groaned. 'Our riding is bound to benefit – if we survive!'

Later that morning, Toni was walking from the stables to the kitchen when she heard Norma's voice floating out of the dining-room's open window.

'Of course, Mother, I've taken care to see that they weren't likely to come to any harm.'

'Oh naturally!' Mrs Gill said in her brittle way.

Toni was about to hurry past the window. Then something almost guilty and defiant in Norma's voice made her forget that she was unintentionally eavesdropping.

'But as you say, Mother,' Norma went on, 'it's got to be done. There's no future in Ponyways so long as it's just a boarding-house for juvenile pony-mads.'

Toni stood quite still.

'Believe me, Mother,' Norma said confidently, 'these children soon won't want to see a saddle again as long as they live. They'll be only too glad to leave Ponyways, and I can guarantee they'll never want to come back! But, all the same, do you think I'm being unfair to Mike in trying to get rid of the children?'

'Fair!' Mrs Gill echoed. 'Of course you're being fair. You're acting in his best interests.'

Toni hurried away. So that was Norma's idea – to ram so much advanced equitation down their throats that they would be sick of ponies.

Well, the sooner she told the others about Norma's plan the better.

CHAPTER XI

—AND LIZ'S COUNTER-PLAN!

That afternoon and evening Norma made her young guests endlessly practise collected walking, trotting and cantering round and round the paddock.

As they went wearily to bed that night, Liz turned to Toni and said feelingly: 'It does seem that Norma is trying to carry out the plan you overheard.'

'Yes, I wonder what she's got in store for us tomorrow,' sighed Toni.

'Something hectic, you can bet,' said Liz, and lapsed into a thoughtful silence.

Heat shimmered from the cobbles in the stable yard as the children led out the saddled and bridled ponies after breakfast next morning.

'Today's going to be a scorcher,' said Pete, blinking up at the blazing sun.

'Not too hot for an endurance ride,' Norma said heartily, leading Destiny from her loose box.

'Have a heart, Norma,' begged Toni. 'By midday it'll be ninety in the shade.'

'I can't help that,' Norma said. 'I've arranged an intensive programme, and we can't let the weather upset it. Now this is the plan. The route is cross-country to High Barrow, following the Pilgrims' Path. You all know the way.'

'But it's all up-hill,' protested Molly, 'and there's not a bit of shade.'

'I said it was an endurance ride,' Norma said, gathering up Destiny's reins and mounting. 'Come on. I'll set the pace.

You'll find I shall press on hard just to show you that it can be done. But I'll wait for you at the Pack Horse Bridge.' She turned in the saddle. 'And don't keep me waiting too long.'

She trotted out of the stable yard, through the wicket gateway that led to the chalky path to the Downs, and cantered off in a cloud of dust, soon leaving the others quite a way behind.

'We'll never keep up,' puffed Gerry, urging Samba with his heels.

'Don't even try to,' said Liz. 'Let her get out of sight. I've got a better plan for a hot day.'

Norma looked to make sure they were following, and then disappeared over the brow of the hill.

'Pull up, everybody!' Liz called, taking charge. 'We're going back to Ponyways to get our swimming things and some sandwiches. The only sensible place to be in a heat-wave is on the beach.'

'Jolly good idea, Liz!' said Cherry. 'Let Norma have her own private endurance test as she's so keen on it.'

'Why not?' agreed Rosemary. 'After all she was only trying to make fools of us.'

Dave chuckled. 'And now it'll be her turn to look silly.'

Half an hour later the young riders, with Candy and Floss bounding eagerly alongside, trotted down the lane to the beach. They turned the ponies into a field where there was some shade and split up to change amid the sandhills.

Soon they were running across the firm sand into the warm shallows and throwing themselves into the sea where Candy and Floss were already swimming after drifts of seaweed.

Liz, Toni and Pete, who were the best swimmers, struck out for the Table Rock and lay basking on its flat surface. By the time they were ready to come back to shore, the tide had dropped so much that they had to swim only about fifteen yards and then they waded through the shallow warm water over the sandy bay.

For the rest of the morning they lay in the sun. Soon, with Candy and Floss competing to catch the bits of sandwich that were thrown for them, they ate their lunch and wondered – some of them apprehensively – whether Norma was enjoying her solo endurance test.

Nine miles away Norma waited astride Destiny near a hump-back bridge. Impatiently she looked at her watch. Ten past one! Really even the slowest riders should have been here by now. She had been waiting almost an hour.

It was too late now for the young riders to return to Pony-ways – by the short-cut along the river bank as far as the creek and then along the shore – in time to get their lunch. Well, they would have to go hungry. It was their own fault for being so slow. The annoying thing was that she, too, felt hungry. There was no chance whatever of getting a meal anywhere round here – and goodness knows how much longer she would have to wait in this heat for those laggards.

'Poor Norma!' sighed Fay, taking a bite out of a cool cucumber sandwich. 'Here we are, gorging, and having a lovely time on the beach while she's probably hot and hungry, waiting by the Pack Horse Bridge.'

'Save your pity!' advised Liz, breaking a chocolate biscuit in two for Candy and Floss. 'I'm enjoying myself too much to let my conscience trouble me.'

Pete got to his feet and stretched.

'Look,' he said. 'The tide's now so low that we could ride the ponies across to Seal Island.'

'Good idea,' said Dave. 'We needn't bother to change out of our swim-suits. Then it won't matter if we do get splashed.'

The ponies enjoyed being ridden over the sands, with the sea-breeze ruffling their manes. Candy and Floss led the way, splashing through the salty rivulets and putting the herring gulls to flight.

Soon the ponies were up to their hocks in a deep gully. They reached a sandbank, and while the dogs were shaking themselves, began to canter towards the shingly beach of Seal Island.

'We've made it,' said Pete, dismounting.

They led their ponies up the grassy slope and across the island to the cliffs. There, below them, were some seals, basking on the rocks.

Puffins scuttled to their burrows or dived into the sea, frightened by the approach of dogs and ponies.

'Isn't it wonderful?' sighed Liz, watching a furry baby seal flopping from a rock into the sea to join its mother.

'This is a marvellous place,' said Cherry. 'I could stay here for hours!'

'Yes, and that's exactly what we'll have to do if we don't start back right away.' Pete pointed to the tide which had turned and was now lapping over the sands, and pouring up the gully. 'Hurry, or we'll be cut off.'

He vaulted on to Black Boy and led the way back across the island to the shingly beach.

They had to swim the ponies across the gully: then the water was only fetlock deep and it was fun splashing through it while Candy and Floss chased each other, and the sun made rainbows in their spray.

Suddenly Gerry gave a shout of alarm.

'Help! Oh, somebody do something! Samba's sinking!'

Toni wheeled Catkin and almost collided with Liz on Barney as they cantered towards the soft patch of sand in which Samba was floundering.

'Keep back, everybody!' Pete warned. 'Gerry, get off and give Samba his head.'

Relieved of Gerry's weight the black pony splashed and bucked his way to firm sand. A mud-spattered Gerry followed.

'Gracious!' Liz exclaimed as she heard other mushy hoofbeats across the sand. 'Here comes more trouble. Norma!'

'What on earth do you all think you're doing?' Norma demanded, jumping off Destiny at the fringe of the soft sand.

'Poor Samba – almost drowned in a quicksand! Of all the irresponsible, ill-mannered, unreliable adolescents – you people really are the limit! What are you doing here anyway?'

'We decided it was too hot for an endurance test,' said Liz, unable to resist the temptation to add to Norma's annoyance.

'So I suppose you decided to cool off the ponies in the sea, and nearly drowned them! Just look at those bridles!' Norma exclaimed. 'Soggy with sea-water. They'll have to be saddle-soaped and oiled. But that's the least of it!' She gazed round at them angrily. 'Think of me riding in this heat, and waiting at the Pack Horse Bridge for hours. Goodness knows what Mike's going to say when he hears about this.'

Cherry, Rosemary and Fay looked at each other uneasily.

'Is there any need for Mike to know?' Pete asked.

'Of course he'll have to know,' Norma declared. 'It's time he learnt what tiresome, ungracious children you are, and how you're ruining Ponyways. Yes, if it wasn't for you lot, Ponyways could be the most famous horse-breaking establishment in the country. Mike and I could turn out show-jumpers by the score. With Mike's reputation there'd be no limit to our success, and instead —' she turned her eyes skywards, 'he has to waste his skill and patience and the whole of Ponyways' resources to teach a crowd of stupid, ungrateful, *tatty* adolescents to ride. Well, wait until I tell him about this; that's all. Perhaps he'll change his mind, and decide that you're not worth bothering about.'

'Eleven, twelve, thirteen, fourteen,' Liz silently counted to prevent herself exploding.

'If you tell Mike about this, Norma,' Toni said quietly, 'we'll have to explain to him why we didn't go on your endurance ride.'

'What exactly do you mean?' Norma asked, baffled and exasperated.

'I overheard you talking to Mrs Gill,' Toni said. 'You told her you were going to ram ponies and horses down our throats until we never wanted to see Ponyways again.'

'We all thought it was a rather mean way of getting your

own ends, Mrs Dashmore,' Pete added.

'*Twenty!*' Liz said aloud to everyone's surprise. 'Yes, Mrs Dashmore, if you tell Mike about us we shall make sure he knows just what you had in mind.'

'You're quite welcome to tell Mike,' Norma shrugged. 'But I don't see what good it's going to do you. Mike already knows exactly how I feel. Anyway he told me this morning that he wants to arrange some of your pony activities himself. I hope that suits you!'

'Suits me anyway!' Liz murmured under her breath as Norma turned Destiny and rode towards Ponyways.

CHAPTER XII

LIKE A BAD PENNY

Next morning after breakfast Mike was sitting in his wheel-chair on the terrace when the postman handed him the letters.

'Is there anything for us, Mike?' asked Gerry Jollison when he and his twin, George, came running from the stables.

'Most of them are for you.' Mike smiled up at them as he guessed the reason for their bumper post. 'Many happy returns of the day!'

'Thanks, Mike.'

'Happy birthday, twins!' chorused Dave, Fay and Molly who had come round from the stables after seeing the postman cycling off down the drive.

'Yippee!' approved Gerry, opening one envelope after another. 'We asked our parents, aunts, and uncles to give us money this year, and they have!'

'Postal orders galore!' announced George. 'Now we'll be able to buy a petrol-driven model plane.'

'And we'll all celebrate by having a party tea,' decided Fay. 'I'll bake a cake.'

'And I'll ice it,' offered Molly.

Later, while Norma was exercising and schooling Destiny on the sands, Mike and the others planned an impromptu gymkhana.

They carried chairs into the paddock for mounted musical bumps, made an obstacle-race course, brought buckets and a sack of potatoes for the potato-sticking race, and set up a course for the 'touch-and-out' jumping competition in which any competitor whose pony touched an obstacle would be eliminated until only the winner would be left.

*

Soon after three o'clock that afternoon, while everybody was busy at the gymkhana, a slim, yellow-haired boy – Robin Gill – was being driven up to the gates of Ponyways.

He flashed a smile at the silver-haired old gentleman who owned the magnificent car which, with an elegant wave of his hand, he had stopped a couple of hours earlier, as it crossed Waterloo Bridge towards the south bank.

Robin now half-bowed to the elderly owner of the Rolls.

'Thank you so much,' he said, in his most charming voice. 'I do hope I haven't taken you too much out of your way.'

'Delighted!' said the old gentleman. 'It's been a pleasant change to have such lively company. It's a tedious journey from London, and you've brightened it for an old man.'

'Thank you, sir,' Robin murmured, taking his cue to act the unassuming, but pleasantly good-mannered youth. 'I'm most grateful.'

Meanwhile, in the paddock, Mike was calling Dave out of the line-up for the potato-race.

'Where's your crash-cap, Dave?' Mike wanted to know.

'Gosh, Mike! I must have left it in my bedroom,' said Dave.

'Your skull may be thick,' Mike said. 'But all the same, I'm not going to risk your fracturing it. Go and fetch your cap. You can compete in a later heat.'

A few moments later, as Dave ran through the kitchen doorway, he met Robin Gill strolling into the hall.

'So you've come back!' Dave gasped, staring at the older boy. 'I say, you're due for a terrific rocket from Mike.'

'Oh, about borrowing those oddments, you mean?' Robin countered calmly. 'That's what I've come back about.'

'You mean you've brought the things back?' asked Dave. 'And Mike's money?'

'Naturally.' Robin smiled disarmingly. 'What do you take me for? A thief?'

'Oh, no of course not,' Dave said quickly. 'I say does anybody expect you?'

'Well, no.' Robin looked round. 'Where is everybody?'

'Your mother and sister are down on the beach,' Dave told him, 'and Mike and the others are in the paddock. I've just come back for my crash cap.'

Robin seemed thoughtful. 'Look, Dave,' he said after a moment, 'don't tell anyone you've seen me.'

'Why not?'

Robin hesitated. 'Well, you see I think it might be better if I had a private word with Mother and Norma before everyone gangs up on me.'

'P'raps so.' Dave nodded. 'But I expect you'll stay to the party, won't you?'

'What party?' asked Robin.

'It's George's and Gerry's birthday,' explained Dave. 'Fay's made a cake and we're going to have an absolutely wizard tea-party.'

'Good!' said Robin. 'Then I'll see everyone at tea. Until then, just don't happen to mention that you've seen me. Savvy?'

Dave was already half-way up the stairs.

'It sounds a bit nutty to me,' he said over his shoulder. 'But if that's the way you want it, fair enough!'

Back in the field the gymkhana was a great success. Dave joined his heat for the potato-race. Each rider had six potatoes in a pile. At a whistle-blast from Mike five riders galloped their ponies down the field. Each rider tried to 'spear' one of the potatoes from the pile with a sharpened stick. Then the riders had to turn their ponies, gallop back, drop the potato in a bucket and return for another one.

Dave was doing well. He had already speared five potatoes, and was galloping down the field for the sixth. With a good aim he speared the potato through the middle. Then the pony that he was riding snatched his bit, threw up his head, cleared the fence at the end of the field and galloped round the far meadow. Dave was out of the race.

Gerry won the heat, and went on to win. After that – musical chairs! Fay won by riding slowly and deliberately, watching each chair, and being prepared to dismount and occupy a vacant one when the music stopped as Mike lifted the pick-up arm of the gramophone. The other competitors rode wildly, and had trouble turning their mounts to reach the chairs quickly enough. There was a scramble of wheeling and jibbing ponies, while Fay calmly walked Russet to a vacant chair, jumped off and sat down.

At last, hot but happy, the ponies were taken back to the stables, rubbed down and fed. Everybody flocked indoors for the birthday tea. Mrs Gill, now back from the beach, poured out from the silver tea-pots – polished for the occasion – and Norma helped to hand round the sandwiches.

'Who's missing?' she asked as she saw a vacant place.

'My other half – Gerry,' said George Jollison. 'He went upstairs to get a handkerchief.'

A moment later, George burst anxiously into the room.

'Our birthday money!' He glanced wildly round at everybody. 'Gosh, George!' He caught his twin's eye, and his voice became a heart-broken wail. 'It's gone! Every single postal order's missing.'

'Oh, no!' echoed George.

'Yes,' miserably affirmed Gerry. 'While I was upstairs I thought I'd count the money again just to make sure that we'd got enough for the model plane. The postal orders should have been in the right-hand top drawer where I left them. But they'd gone.'

'Are you sure you didn't put them anywhere else?' Mike questioned.

'Absolutely,' George confirmed. 'They were in the top right-hand drawer of the dressing-table – just as Gerry says.'

'Well!' Norma said smoothly. 'If there is someone light-fingered among us no one can blame Robin this time. He's miles away in London.'

'But he isn't!' Dave declared and explained how he had seen Robin in the hall an hour ago.

'Robin here!' Mrs Gill lifted a slice of lemon from her tea and let the spoon drop into the saucer with a tinkle. 'Oh, my poor boy!'

'He can't be far away,' said Mike. He turned to his young guests. 'Split up and look for him. He must be found at once.'

'I won't have you persecuting my boy in this way.' It was Mrs Gill's turn to wail. 'You haven't a shadow of proof.'

'It's no use, Mummy,' Norma moved to her mother and stood soothingly by her chair. 'I've told Mike about Robin. He understands.'

'I'm hanged if I do!' Mike groaned. 'This is getting beyond a joke. The boy's a kleptomaniac.'

'No, Mike, he's not,' Mrs Gill protested. 'How can you say such a thing? Robin must be in desperate trouble, or he wouldn't have borrowed this money.'

'Borrowed!' Mike echoed indignantly. 'That's just the trouble, Mother. It's because you haven't faced facts about him that Robin's in this kind of mess. He steals – and the sooner you realize it the better for Robin.' He broke off as Pete and Liz came back. 'Any sign of him?'

'No, Mike,' said Liz.

Just then Gerry panted into the room. 'Robin was seen hailing Lord Carelon's Daimler half an hour ago on the London road,' he reported 'The man with the tractor in that field opposite the paddock spotted him.'

'Robin certainly believes in travelling in style!' sighed Norma.

'To think that he's left without a word to his mother!' Mrs Gill wafted a scented handkerchief towards her brow. She looked up at Norma. 'I don't understand him at all.'

'I do,' Mike said grimly. 'He got a quick haul, and made a quick getaway.' He took a wallet from his pocket. 'Here, twins. I'll pay back your birthday money, and I'll settle up with Master Robin later. Now, how much did your postal orders add up to?'

'Seven pounds fifty,' Gerry said. 'But we don't want to take

your money, Mike. We'll wait until you get it back from Robin.'

'You'll do nothing of the sort.' Mike pressed the notes into his hand. 'Now, nip upstairs and put the money away safely.' He turned to the others. 'If anybody sees Robin anywhere round here again he's to come straight to me, understand?' His voice became softer as he realized that Mrs Gill was weeping. 'Sorry, Mother.'

Mrs Gill glared at her son-in-law through tear-filled eyes. 'You're hard, Mike. Hard!' she accused unjustly.

'Robin should have got back to London by now,' Mike told Norma after supper that evening. 'I think we ought to have a word with him.' He propelled his wheel-chair to the study, and picked up the telephone. 'I'll ask Directory Enquiries to look up the telephone number of these Charteris people in Kegan Square.'

A quarter of an hour later he was talking to Robin's friend, Charteris.

'May I speak to Robin Gill, please? ... He's not there? Do you know where he's gone? ... You don't ... Well, my name's Mike Dashmore. I'm Robin's brother-in-law ... What's that? ...' Mike listened for a while. 'I see!' he commented grimly. 'Well, please telephone me if you get any news. Marling 540. Thank you. Good-bye.'

'Well,' said Norma, sitting on the edge of the study desk and looking anxiously at her husband. 'What's the bad news?'

'Charteris is after Robin's blood,' explained Mike. 'It seems that Robin walked out of the flat this morning with three pounds belonging to him, and two ties, a check shirt and a pair of jeans belonging to another boy from the flat upstairs.'

Norma shuddered slightly.

'How dreadful! And for you, too!' She tried to pull herself together as she felt Mike's comforting hand on her arm. 'We've got to face it. Robin's nothing more than a juvenile delinquent.

He'll have to be taught a sharp lesson. Though goodness knows how!'

'If Robin had been more interested in ponies,' Liz said to Toni next morning, 'he might not have become such a bad hat.'

'I wonder what he really is interested in – if anything,' Toni mused as she leaned on the five-barred gate and looked across at the young, unbroken horses which were grazing in the lower meadow. 'Oh, let's try to forget about him! Hullo!' She broke off as she saw a Rolls Royce coming up the drive. 'Who's this?'

'Winton Blare and his wife, of all people!' exclaimed Liz. 'Come on, Toni. I'll introduce you to them.'

'But I look a sight,' protested Toni. 'Quite tatty, as Norma would say.'

'The Winton Blares won't worry about that,' Liz assured her. 'They're poppets.'

'Hi, there!' Sadie Blare stepped out of the car. 'Why, Liz! You're just the girl I wanted to see. And this is one of the other Ponyways' guests, huh?'

'Miss O'Neil – I mean, Mrs Blare, may I introduce Toni?' Liz said.

'So this is Toni,' Sadie said warmly. 'I've heard about you from Liz, and, for land's sake! – drop the Miss O'Neil, both of you, and the Mrs Blare. I guess I'm Sadie to my friends, now as always.' She turned as Winton Blare got out of the car, with portly dignity, followed by a keen-eyed young man who had a jaunty brown beard. 'Winton, dear, and Bruno, honey, this is Liz's friend, Toni.' Sadie took Toni's arm and drew her forward. 'Now, Bruno —' she turned to the young man with the beard '— don't you agree this is just a swell set-up for your programme?'

'But definitely yes.' The young man named Bruno nodded enthusiastically.

'You see,' Sadie explained to Toni and Liz, 'the B.B.C. want to do a programme about Ponyways on the television *At Home* series. Please take us to Mike Dashmore so that we can have a talk about it.'

CHAPTER XIII

ROBIN SPRINGS A SURPRISE

'Ponyways on T.V.!' Norma exclaimed after Winton and Sadie Blare, and Bruno Maxwell, had told her and Mike about their idea. She walked across the drawing-room to Mike's side. 'Why, Mike, this really will set the seal of success on our plan to train young horses. We'll be able to concentrate on that in the programme, and keep the children out of the way.'

'No, honey!' Sadie protested. 'It's not the horse-breaking that we want to televise. We'd like to show Ponyways from the angle of the young guests. We'll want kids all over the place, in jeans and jodhs, just being natural, riding their ponies, and rampaging around the house – you know.'

'But that's how Ponyways really is!' sighed Norma. 'Rather a nightmare!'

'Oh, Liz!' Mrs Gill opened the door of her attic bed-sittingroom, and called down the stairs. 'Who are all these people? Am I needed?'

'I don't think so, Mrs Gill,' Liz shouted back. 'They're from the B.B.C. Mike and Norma are dealing with them.'

'B.B.C.,' Mrs Gill echoed. 'Really! Well, I think I certainly ought to see them.'

Mrs Gill was crossing the first landing when there was a ring from the front doorbell.

'Liz!' she called, as Liz was now half-way to the kitchen. '*Door!*'

Liz opened the front door to see a tall man in a raincoat and trilby hat.

'Good morning,' the man said, stepping into the hall. 'I want to see Robin Gill, please.'

'But he isn't here,' said Liz.

'Then perhaps you could tell me where I can find him,' the man suggested firmly.

'He may be in London,' said Liz.

The man was about to ask another question when Mrs Gill reached the front door.

'Please, Liz,' she said quietly, and Liz was surprised to hear how strained Mrs Gill suddenly sounded. 'I'll talk to this gentleman.' She turned to the stranger. 'Come this way.' She walked towards the study, and before she shut the door, Liz heard her say to the man: 'I'm Robin's mother.'

Ten minutes later the study door opened. Mrs Gill, pale and tense, showed the stranger to the front door. After he had gone she paused in the hall for a moment as though to pull herself together, and then she walked to the drawing-room.

'Something dreadful's happened!' she announced, and broke off as she saw that her daughter and son-in-law were not alone. 'I didn't realize that you B.B.C. people were still here. Norma, Mike – I must have a word with you immediately.'

Sadie moved from the chimney-piece and linked arms with Winton and Bruno.

'We were about to do a fade-out anyway,' she said tactfully. She turned to Norma. 'We'll telephone you and make another date to talk over the final details.'

As soon as Bruno and the Blares had gone, Mrs Gill sank on to the sofa and began quietly to weep.

Norma sat beside her mother and put an arm round her to comfort her. Mike turned his wheel-chair to face them both.

'Steady on, Mother,' said Norma. 'What's happened?'

'The police are looking for Robin.' She caught at Mike's arm. 'A detective-sergeant has just been here.'

'Good gracious!' exclaimed Norma. 'This is what I've dreaded.'

'Go on,' Mike quietly said to his mother-in-law.

'Someone's made a complaint against Robin – some wretched man who is making out that Robin got money out of him by false pretences.'

Norma's breath caught.

'Do you mean to say that Robin will be brought into court?'

Mike looked worried. 'He'd have to be dealt with in the police court.'

'Don't!' moaned Mrs Gill. 'I can't stand it. There's no question of the police taking any such action. I've seen to that.'

'How?' Mike wanted to know.

'I told the detective to send the wretched man to me so that I could pay him any money that Robin may have borrowed.'

Mike leaned forward.

'And what did the detective-sergeant say about that?'

'I can't recollect that he said anything.' Mrs Gill was thoughtful. 'He seemed to let me do most of the talking.'

'I can imagine that,' said Norma. 'It's probably a way that detectives have.'

Mike stirred restlessly in his wheel-chair. 'If I wasn't chained to this confounded thing I'd go to London, track down Robin and find out what it's all about.'

Norma got to her feet. 'I'll go. First I'll try the Charteris's flat, and get a lead from there.'

'Yes, do that.' Mrs Gill crumpled her handkerchief. 'Find my son and bring him back here. We can't have him wandering loose in London, getting into more trouble.'

'I'll take the shooting-brake and go right away.' Norma was already at the door.

'Perhaps I ought to come with you,' Mrs Gill suggested, still distressed.

'No, Mother.' Norma was firm. 'I can handle Robin better on my own.'

'As soon as you find him, telephone me.' Mrs Gill managed to pull herself together. 'And – oh, Norma! – not a word about this to any of those tiresome children. They already know too much about our private affairs as it is.'

*

Soon after nine o'clock next morning, before Mrs Gill was downstairs, the telephone bell rang in the study.

Liz, a dish-mop in her hand, hurried from the kitchen to answer it.

'Is that Ponyways?' asked a care-free young voice. 'This is Robin Gill. May I speak to Norma?'

Liz gripped the receiver in surprise.

'Norma isn't here,' Liz told him, trying to be polite. 'She went off yesterday in the shooting-brake with a suitcase. I suppose Mike and your mother must know where she is now, but nobody's bothered to tell us.'

'I dare say she's gone to buy some more wild horses,' Robin drawled. 'Never mind.' He paused for thought. 'Listen, Liz. Don't bother to tell Mike or my mother that I've phoned. They'd only flap.'

'I know!' said Liz, and then decided that there was no point in hiding her anger. 'Everyone's furious with you – including me. You really are a horror to take the twins' birthday money! Why don't you come back and pay up?'

'I can pay the money back – yes, and with interest,' Robin said indignantly. 'But I can't come to Ponyways yet. I'm too busy in London.'

'What are you doing?' Liz asked, as the operator's voice broke in.

'Your three minutes are up, caller. Please insert another ten pence if you require another three minutes.'

'I'm just ringing off now, operator,' Robin said quickly. 'Listen, Liz. I want you and some of the others to come to London tomorrow. Be at the New Coffee Bean, just behind Baker Street station, at three o'clock. I promise you the surprise of your lives. But mind – not a word to the grown-ups! Understand?'

'I am cutting you off now, caller!' interrupted the operator, and the line went dead.

CHAPTER XIV

ROBIN'S DOWNFALL

'What's Robin up to?' wondered Liz as she, Toni, Fay, Rosemary and Pete waited on the up-platform of Drayfield railway station next morning. 'And why does he want to see us? If only that operator hadn't cut us off!'

'I can't make up my mind,' said Pete, 'whether he really is a bad hat or just scatty.'

Fay was worried. 'I think we ought to have told Mike and Mrs Gill all about Robin wanting us to go to London to see him instead of just saying we were going for a pony-less picnic.'

'Why should we have to account for all our movements?' rebelled Liz. 'After all, Norma hasn't come back yet, and no one's told us where she's gone to. Hullo! Here's the train now.'

They found a carriage to themselves and immediately began to eat their sandwiches.

At Victoria station they changed to the Underground, and, just before ten minutes to three, they came out into the sunlight among the bustle of traffic and pedestrians at a corner of Baker Street.

'All points West to Madame Tussauds and the London Zoo,' Pete said breezily. 'Now what and where is the New Coffee Bean?'

'First on the right, second on the left, chum,' obliged a newspaper seller.

A few minutes later they all stared at a frontage, boldly painted in red and gold, with jazzy neon lettering.

'The New Coffee Bean,' read Toni.

'It's a coffee bar!' exclaimed Liz.

'Suffering star-gazers!' Pete gasped, walking to a glaring poster. 'Just look at this.'

They crowded round to read scarlet lettering on a vivid yellow background.

ROBIN ROCK, King of the Roll, appearing Nightly. Prior to Three Weeks at the Café du Continent.

Under the lettering was pasted a glossy full-length photograph of a youth in tight jeans and a check shirt. His fair hair was long, and flopped over his forehead. He was pictured in the act of strumming a guitar.

'It's Robin!' Liz gasped.

'Gosh!' said Pete. 'Has he rocked 'n' rolled his way to stardom overnight?'

'And, heaven help us, here he comes – in person!' said Toni, as the glass doors of the coffee bar swung open, and a real-life, Technicolor version of the photograph walked jauntily towards them.

'Well! Well! So this is your latest stunt, Robin!' Pete exclaimed. 'I read somewhere that rock 'n' roll was on its way out, but perhaps you'll be able to prolong the craze.'

'For long enough to cash in and pay back your "borrowings",' Liz said meaningly.

'*Touché!*' Robin acknowledged with a charming smile. He delved a hand into one of the pockets of his jeans, and brought out several pieces of crumpled paper.

'Fivers!' Fay exclaimed.

Robin counted out three, and handed them to Liz. 'That will cover what I owe at Ponyways,' he told her.

'If there's any change,' said Liz, putting the money safely into her shoulder bag, 'I'll see that you have it later.'

Robin shrugged. 'Chicken feed!' He gestured towards the poster and photograph as though to infer that the phenomenal success of his rocking 'n' rolling would immediately put him in the hundred-pound-a-week class. 'Come in, everybody. I'll give you a pre-view of the routine that I am doing at the Café du Continent.'

They followed Robin. At the far end of the coffee bar was a small stage where three youths, also in jeans and check shirts, sat on stools, at a piano, double-bass and drums.

Robin leapt on the stage, and picked up his guitar. At a signal from him the other youths broke into a frenzy of sound while Robin, strumming his guitar, and shouting out the words, swayed and rocked around the stage.

'I'm gonna rock around the clock tonight,' Robin intoned. *'Gonna rock, rock, rock in the bright moonlight!'*

Every gesture that Robin made was greeted with delighted shrieks from two teenage girls who served behind the counter of the coffee bar.

'Ooooh! He's wonderful!' sighed one of the girls.

'When Robin rocks, oh, my, my!' swooned the other one.

The music reached a faster tempo, and now Robin was chanting so quickly that it was difficult to hear the words. He straddled the stage, a slim, be-jeaned figure, plucking still wilder chords from his guitar. Then he gave a primeval, jungle call, and with a final leap ended the number.

Liz felt that the silence which followed was a blessed relief, but it was broken all too soon by the two girls behind the counter clapping wildly.

'More, Robin!' one called.

'Well, what do you think of it, ponies?' Robin asked, jumping down from the stage to join Liz, Fay, Toni, Rosemary and Pete.

'I've never seen anything quite like it before,' Toni said with tactful honesty.

'I have,' said Pete, 'on the films, and on the television, and I think you're every bit as good as any of the other rock 'n' rollers.'

'Whatever made you take it up?' asked Fay.

'I had a guitar when I was in digs before I came to London, and I used to play a bit of rock 'n' roll then,' explained Robin. 'But it wasn't until I read what a lot of money a rock 'n' roll star can earn that I decided to make a career of it.'

Liz gave a meaning look. 'I can understand your wanting to start at the top. That's just like you.'

'Why not?' said Robin. 'If I'm no good I can always work my way down.'

'I thought that the hire-purchase people took back your guitar,' said Pete.

'So they did,' nodded Robin. 'That's why I had to buy another one. The cash that I'd borrowed from the twins wasn't enough, so I had to get some from the hall porter of the block of flats where Charteris lives. I couldn't borrow any more from Charteris because we'd already had a row about money. As a matter of fact he more or less booted me out. It was a bit of luck that he did because that's why I wandered in here. I read a card in a newsagent's window that there was a bedroom to let over the New Coffee Bean. So I took it, and the other night I gave a turn on the stage, and right away I was spotted by a talent scout —'

Robin's voice trailed off into a worried monotone as a trilby-hatted man pushed open the swing door of the coffee bar. The boy's jaw dropped. Then he deliberately turned his back on the stranger, and forced a jaunty confidence.

'No more borrowing by me,' he told the others. 'I'm a reformed character. Rockin' Robin is going to do right by all. And I'm going to start by buying a hat-shop for Mother so that she won't have to stay at Ponyways.'

'Mike will appreciate that!' Liz said almost inaudibly, and then broke off as the trilby-hatted man stood stolidly in front of Robin.

'Is your name Robin Gill?' asked the man.

Robin gulped. 'It is.'

'I am a police officer,' announced the man, and took out a notebook. 'A Mr Horace Watts, employed as a hall porter at Rookwood Mansions, Kegan Place, has filed a complaint, alleging that you have obtained from him the sum of ten pounds by false pretences.'

'False pretences!' Robin echoed indignantly. 'What rot! I only borrowed the money. I was going to pay it back this evening.'

'Yes, that's right, officer,' said Pete. 'He's got the money on him now – money that he has earned himself. Show him, Robin.'

The plain-clothes man looked blank as Robin brought out some crumpled five-pound notes.

'Look, officer,' Liz said persuasively, 'it does seem a pity to ruin Robin's big chance. I know he's done wrong, and so does he. But he's turning over a new leaf, and he's making himself quite famous as a rock 'n' roller.'

The plain-clothes man seemed unimpressed.

'He'll have the chance to explain any extenuating circumstances to the magistrate,' he said. He turned to Robin. 'Now I must ask you to accompany me to the police station.'

'Oh, have a heart!' pleaded Robin. 'Couldn't we take a taxi at my cxpense, and pay back the hall porter so that he'd withdraw the charges?'

'I'm afraid not, Mr Gill,' said the police officer. 'You'll have the chance to offer restitution when you're brought up before the magistrate, and that should be a point in your favour.'

'Magistrate, indeed!' Robin echoed. 'Whatever next?' He glared at the police officer. 'Yes, I will come to the police station with you – to have a word with your superior.'

The police officer froze.

'Very well, sir,' he said stiffly. 'This way.'

Robin followed the plain-clothes man to the door, and then turned to wave jauntily to everyone in the coffee bar.

'Don't go away, ponies,' he told Liz and Co. 'I'll be back in a few moments. See you later, alligators!'

'So long, wonder-boy!' called out the eldest of the rock 'n' roll instrumentalists, who was jealous of Robin's easy success. 'We'll try to get by without you. One – er, two.' He gave the signal to the other musicians to speed Robin on his way to the police station with rhythm. 'Robin's gonna rock around the dock tomorrow!'

'Stow it!' Pete growled at the youths.

'Look!' exclaimed Liz pointing to a green shooting-brake that was drawing up at the kerb outside the New Coffee Bean. Liz and Co. gasped in surprise as Norma got out and entered the coffee bar.

Norma blinked in amazement when she saw Liz and the others.

'Good gracious!' she exclaimed. 'What are you all doing here? I've been tracking down Robin. Where is he?'

'Prepare yourself for a shock, Norma,' Liz said quietly, and explained exactly what had happened. '... And so your brother went off with the plain-clothes man to the police station.'

'To see the police officer's superior, if you please,' chipped in the jealous musician. 'That'll make him popular. I don't think!'

'Oh dear!' groaned Norma. 'I'd better go along there.'

'You can't miss it,' obliged the double-bass player. 'Second on the left, third on the right. Follow the blue lamp to Robin Rock, king of the Roll.'

Pete touched Norma's shoulder.

'Would you like us to come along with you, Norma?' he asked quietly.

'No, thanks, Pete.' Norma was already half-way to the door. 'I really think you all ought to get back to Ponyways on the next train. I shan't be able to give you a lift because goodness only knows when I'll be getting back. This may take a lot of sorting out, and I may have to see a lawyer.'

CHAPTER XV

AND THEN – TELEVISION

'It wouldn't have helped even if you and Mother had come to London, Mike,' Norma said when she got back to Ponyways just before tea next day. 'I engaged a good lawyer, and Robin was only in front of the magistrate for about two minutes this morning while the lawyer asked for the case to be put back for a week.'

'That should give the lawyer a chance to work up somc kind of defence,' nodded Mike.

'But why didn't you bring Robin back with you, Norma?' asked Mrs Gill. 'Where is he now?'

'He's got a bedroom over the coffee bar where he's working,' explained Norma. 'He couldn't come away without giving up his so-called job there.'

'So he's still rocking 'n' rolling,' mused Mike from his wheel-chair. 'I must say he's absolutely undeflatable!'

'What'll happen to Robin?' Gerry Jollison asked at breakfast next morning.

'I say!' His twin looked up with a bright and happy smile. 'Do you think he'll be sent to prison?'

'I shouldn't think so,' said Liz. 'But anyway I'm tired of talking about Robin. We shan't know his fate for a week, so for the time being I vote we concentrate on something more worthwhile. Does anyone know what time the B.B.C. Film Unit is coming this morning?'

'Mike said around ten,' said Dave. 'You know, when you come to think of it, these T.V. programmes need a lot of preparation. I suppose they're going to film some of the riding scenes so that they can suddenly switch from indoor scenes to outdoor ones during the actual programme.'

'Yes, from a live broadcast to the film,' nodded Pete. 'You see this programme will be going out at eight o'clock in the evening. That will be all right for interior shots because I suppose they'll have big lamps round the house, but, outside, the daylight might not be strong enough.'

'Or it might be raining, or a sea mist might sweep in,' put in Gerry. 'I think it's a good idea that they're going to film some of the sequences. It means we'll be able to see ourselves on the television.'

'I hadn't thought of that!' Liz said soberly. 'I bet I'll look a sight.' She shrugged. 'Ah well, it can't be helped.'

'If you really feel like that, Liz,' Norma said, entering the kitchen, 'you needn't be in the film. I think it might not be a bad idea for anyone who doesn't feel *telegenic* to tackle some of the other jobs – helping to get a cold lunch for the B.B.C. people, for instance.'

Leaving Liz pink with humiliation, Norma went to the stables where Toni and Cherry were polishing tack. She picked up a leather, glossed her already immaculate boots and went to Destiny's box.

'Oh, Toni,' she called. 'I wonder if you could come here for a moment. I think Destiny's tail should be washed, don't you? It always makes a grey look so much better. And Cherry, if you would just oil her hooves. I don't want to get myself dirty.'

When at last Destiny shone to Norma's satisfaction she mounted the mare and rode her to the far paddock. Soon afterwards Winton Blare's Rolls Royce drew up. Sadie and Winton got out. Next came a Cadillac with bearded Bruno Maxwell and another arty young man, unbearded but with longish hair. Vans of filming equipment followed, with engineers and cameramen, belonging to the B.B.C. Television Film Unit.

'Everybody ready?' Sadie asked brightly. 'Well, you do look smart. Say!' she looked round puzzled. 'Where's Liz?'

'Liz!' Pete ran into the house and called frantically. 'Liz, come on. Everybody's waiting!'

Liz, with a check overall on top of her riding kit, appeared at the kitchen door. Her eyes behind her spectacles looked as if she had been weeping.

'I'm not coming,' she said in a small voice.

'I say, old girl, what's wrong?' Pete asked.

'I'm not in the jumping any more.' Liz turned away. 'That's all. Don't wait for me.'

'What is this?' Sadie appeared behind Pete. 'Say, Liz, what are you doing in that get-up? Come on, honey. Everybody else is ready.'

'I'm not in the film any more,' Liz repeated.

'Why ever not?' Sadie asked. 'What's wrong?'

'I'm not telegenic,' Liz said, straightening her spectacles fiercely. 'You want only the good-looking ones. I shall spoil the film.'

'My dear child!' Sadie was appalled. 'Have you gone crackers? Who said you weren't telegenic, anyway? It's so silly. You look *cute*. Don't you know? You were a hit at the party when you stayed with us overnight.'

'That was different,' said Liz. 'I took off my spectacles for that, but I can't *jump* without them.'

'With or without your specs, honey,' Sadie said emphatically, 'you look fine. Doesn't she?' she turned to Pete.

'She looks O.K. to me?' Pete grunted. Honestly, girls were the end. All this shame-making fuss about looks! 'I can't see anything wrong with her.'

Sadie took Liz's arm. 'Now take off that pinafore and come right outside. We want to start filming.'

The cameras were already in position in the jumping paddock when Norma made a showy entrance on Destiny. Coming into sight across the meadow, she put the mare over the fence into the jumping paddock, cantered up to the first jump and made a clear round of the ring.

'What do you say?' one of the cameramen appealed to Bruno. 'Shall I shoot?'

The B.B.C. producer shook his head. He had decided that Norma's unscheduled appearance was not going to spoil his own plans.

'But look at that action,' the cameraman pointed out. 'It would make a fine opening sequence.'

'I dare say, but it's not going to,' Bruno said definitely. 'When you've quite finished your marathon,' he told Norma as she reined, 'we may be able to get on with the filming.'

'Didn't you film my entrance?' Norma was puzzled. 'I thought it would make a good introduction. After all, your programme's supposed to be about a jumping establishment isn't it?'

'Not about star-jumpers, my dear,' Winton Blare said suavely, as he joined Bruno Maxwell and Norma. 'It's the beginners we want. Remember?'

'Quite!' Bruno looked round. 'Now where are those twins? And that girl with the pig-tails?' He turned to Toni. 'Go and fetch them, quickly. What we would like to film,' he explained to Norma, 'is the learners, falling off, knocking jumps down sometimes. Nothing too perfect.'

Bruno began to tell the riders exactly what were his plans. First there was to be the trotting circle round the paddock. Then the younger riders would complete an easy jumping-course. Afterwards, Liz, Toni, Pete and Cherry were to give a display of bare-back jumping, taking the fences in the jumping lane at their full height.

'Come on everybody,' said Mike, propelling his wheel-chair into the middle of the paddock to direct the riding lesson. 'To horse! Into a circle, all of you. Norma – give them a lead.'

With Norma in front on Destiny, the Ponyway riders began to trot round the paddock. One or two of them felt nervous, and some of the ponies, conscious of the film-cameras, began to buck.

To put the riders at their ease, Mike began to sing the Ponyways trail song:

'Get along, little pony, get along,
I'm happy at Ponyways where I belong.
Oh, I'll ride all day,
In a care free way.
Get along, little pony, get along!'

Happily the children joined in, and soon the ponies were trotting easily, in a rhythmic circle.

'That's terrific!' Bruno said, and turned to the cameramen. 'Shoot!'

CHAPTER XVI

TROUBLE FOR NORMA

'I'm worn out after all that T.V. filming yesterday,' Liz sighed to Cherry, Toni and Molly as they forked the dirty straw from the stables next day. 'I suppose it's the nerve strain of waiting for the programme to be sent out next week, and for Robin's case coming up —'

'And something else, too!' Pete announced, joining them with a pitch-fork to lend a hand. 'Things are certainly piling up at Ponyways. Norma's decided to jump Destiny in the County Show next Tuesday.'

'She must be mad!' Liz pronounced, giving an exasperated swish with her broom. 'Or perhaps she thought she wasn't getting enough limelight yesterday.'

'Miaow!' Cherry warned Liz. She turned to Pete. 'Are you sure about this?'

'Sure as I'm standing here,' Pete said definitely. 'Fay's just gone to post the entry form.'

'It's only a couple of days since Norma told me she wouldn't be ready to enter Destiny in any show until the end of the summer.' Cherry looked puzzled. 'She said that Destiny was a one-man mare since she had been ridden only by Mike for so long, and that she did not seem willing to jump well for anybody else.'

'I suppose Norma's decided that Destiny might have a chance after all,' said Molly. 'But if I were in her place I'd feel rather unhappy.'

'Unhappy!' Cherry echoed. 'Norma hasn't looked particularly happy since Mike broke his leg!'

On the day before the Show Norma hardly ate any lunch.

'I'm nervous,' she admitted, getting up from the table and lighting a fresh cigarette from the stub of the first. 'I think I'll ride Destiny over to Twelvetrees Farm. It will steady her nerves and mine and I'll be able to give her some jumping practice on the way. Besides I want to pick up the raspberry-jelly recipe Mrs Cuddemore promised me. Fay said she'd help me with the jam-making while she's here.'

'I'd love to,' Fay said good-naturedly, pleased by Norma's new interest in domesticity. 'I'll show you how to bottle the pears, too. I always help Mummy with ours.'

Norma set off, and Liz and Toni helped Fay to cut sandwiches for the picnic they had planned for that afternoon while Pete, Dave, and Sheila tackled the dishes. A few minutes later Mike propelled his chair into the kitchen. He had a small flat tin on his knees.

'Oh, Liz,' he said. 'Would you ride after Norma for me and give her this for Mr Cuddemore? His son, William, is coming on leave, and I promised him these trout flies. He wanted to try them on the Turnet stream.'

'Right, Mike.' Liz took the box. 'I'll take Barney.' She turned to the others. 'Don't wait for me. I'll probably ride on to the Roman Camp. See you all at supper-time.'

Barney was glad of a canter. White dust flew from his hooves as he sped up the track to the Downs. On the ridge Liz halted and looked round. There was Norma, down by the chalk pit. No need to hurry. Norma was only riding Destiny at a trot. Barney would soon catch up with them.

Unaware that she was being followed, Norma began to canter Destiny down the hillside. Then she turned off the Downs along a green lane, pushed open a field gate on to the Cuddemores' land and began to jump Destiny over the trim hedges of the meadows that lay between there and Twelvetrees Farm.

Liz galloped Barney after them.

'Come on!' she urged the pony. 'We've got to catch up.'

She was enjoying the ride. Barney was gaining now. She

watched Norma and Destiny taking the stile into a wheat field, and saw them carefully skirting the edge of the crop. Then Destiny rose to jump a post and rails and, next moment, both horse and rider suddenly disappeared.

Liz trotted round the wheat field. She put Barney at the post and rails, and then pulled up short.

There was Norma, huddled on the ground on the other side of the jump, while Destiny grazed a little way off.

Destiny's martingale trailed, broken, on the ground. Norma had lost her cap, and she was now sitting with her elbows on her knees and her hands to her head.

Liz jumped off Barney and ran forward. Destiny must have come down at the fence and thrown Norma.

'Norma, what's wrong?' Liz asked anxiously and then as Norma lifted her head, she saw that she was weeping. 'Are you hurt?'

Norma looked up startled. She quickly brushed the tears from her eyes.

'What do you think you're doing, following me around?' she demanded angrily. 'Am I never to be left alone? Can't I even fall off Destiny without one of you turning up to gloat? Oh, it's the last straw!' She glared at Liz. 'I'm fed up. Go away. Of course I'm not hurt.'

Liz looked at her in bewilderment.

'I'm sorry, Norma,' she began. 'But if you're not hurt, why are you crying?'

'Why?' Norma echoed desperately. 'I'll tell you why! How would you like to marry a grand person like Mike, and come to live at Ponyways only to find that the house is full of adolescents and you never have a moment's peace? Besides the place is impossible to run and I can't get any help.'

'Too bad!' Liz said in a flat voice.

'Yes, I know, you're thinking I was mad to sack Mrs Roylance and Maud,' said Norma. 'But you don't know the half of it. Mrs Roylance had it in for me right from the start. She was always waiting to catch me out. She wanted to show Mike how little I knew about housekeeping. She said critical things because I spent my time riding ... Why shouldn't I ride? I might have been in the British team that went to Spain if I'd stayed single. Oh, I knew before I married Mike that he ran riding holidays and instruction courses at Ponyways, but I thought he delegated a lot of the work. I didn't know we'd have to *slave* – that the house would be disorganized – that we'd never have a moment to ourselves. I thought we'd be able to switch over to horse-breaking and dealing. Well, it seems I was wrong because Mike wants to keep on with the holiday courses. And what with him breaking his leg – and all you children everywhere. It's enough to make an angel weep!'

'I see!' Liz said miserably. 'Of course we could stop coming here if that would help.'

'You must all keep coming here.' Norma got to her feet and brushed herself down. 'It's what Mike wants, and I want him to be happy.' She grabbed Destiny's reins. 'I suppose everything's got too much for me. What with Mummy turning up, and Robin being arrested – well that was the end!'

Liz looked unhappy.

'I wish I could help.'

'No one can,' Norma said hopelessly. 'Nobody can reform Robin or take Mummy off our hands.' She gave Destiny a rueful pat. 'Nor even make this mare forget the grudge she's got against me. You know, Liz,' she went on frankly, 'I was wrong to drive Destiny so hard that day. That's why she doesn't like me.'

'Horses have such long memories.' Liz sighed. 'But, perhaps when she gets to the show-ground the excitement will make her forget her grudge and she'll jump as well as ever.'

'I hope so,' Norma said fervently. She put up a hand to stroke the mare's nose in yet another attempt to make friends. 'Come on, old girl. Forgive me.'

Destiny tossed her head, snorting, and almost jerked the reins from Norma's hands.

'You see,' Norma groaned, turning to Liz. 'It's no use. How can she possibly jump well for anyone she dislikes so much?'

*

'Things haven't happened as we expected,' Norma told Mike when she came in from her ride later that afternoon. 'We both thought that if you kept away from Destiny – and didn't make too much fuss for her – that she'd switch her loyalty to me and work well for me until you were able to ride her yourself. But it hasn't turned out like that. Perhaps she imagines I'm keeping you away from her.'

Mike bit thoughtfully on the stem of his pipe, and then propelled his wheel-chair to the open French window.

'Let's see if I can talk some horse-sense into her,' he suggested.

Norma pushed Mike's wheel-chair across the drive to the paddock gate. Destiny moved slowly from the shade of the far oak tree as she heard their approach. Her ears flicked forward.

'Destiny!' Mike called cheerfully. 'Come here, old girl!'

The mare whinnied, threw up her head and cantered to Mike, standing over him and rubbing her head against his jacket.

'Love me, love my wife, Destiny!' Mike said, making much of the mare. 'I want to see how you're jumping.' He turned to Norma. 'Fetch her saddle and bridle and see if she'll do any better for you while I'm watching.'

Still bemused by Mike's petting, Destiny hardly noticed the bit that Norma slipped into her mouth, nor the weight of the saddle on her back. It was not until Norma put a foot into the stirrup iron, and swung a leg across the mare, that Destiny flattened her left ear, and rolled a quizzical eye at Mike.

'Go on, you big, silly mare!' Mike gave Destiny a fond slap on the neck. 'Jump for her!'

Norma turned the mare and cantered her towards the brushwood fence. Destiny seemed keen. Her stride quickened. She cleared the fence and galloped to take the big spread of the parallel gates. Norma gave the mare her head as she came up to the stile. Destiny soared over, turned the corner at the end of the paddock, and came to extend herself over the water jump.

Showily she cantered past Mike on her way to the in-and-out.

'Keep it up, Destiny!' Mike shouted. 'Good girl!'

Norma hardly dared to hope. Did Destiny really understand that Mike wanted her to do her best? Or was her faultless jumping just a fluke? Destiny was now slowing her pace for the in-and-out, so that she could time the tricky jumps to a nicety. Norma felt the mare's muscles tense as she gathered herself for the first fence. They were half a stride away – now for it!

Just as Destiny took off, Norma caught sight of a piece of jagged metal sticking out of the ground between the two jumps. Instinctively she tugged at the reins. If Destiny took the fence she would land on that metal. It would gash her foot, perhaps laming her for life.

But it was too late now to stop the mare. She was in the air, half-way over the fence.

Desperately Norma threw her weight to the left of the saddle, and tugged at her left rein. Destiny faltered in mid-air, twisted, and knocked over the wing at the side of the jump. She stumbled, missing the piece of metal by inches, and rolled over. Norma was thrown clear. She scrambled to her feet and jerked out of the ground a half-buried piece of a rusty old ploughshare that had worked its way to the surface. She ran to Destiny, grasped her bridle and led her away from the fallen jump.

'I don't suppose you'll ever trust me again after I brought you down like that,' she said, showing the mare the piece of metal. 'But this was why I had to do it.'

'She saved you, Destiny!' Mike said, propelling his chair over the grass. 'If only that mare could understand plain English!' he groaned. 'But—' He broke off. 'By golly – perhaps she does.'

Unexpectedly Destiny had pushed her head forward and licked Norma's chin. Next moment the mare bunted Norma's shoulder and threw up her head to give a pleased whinny.

'Hey, steady on!' Norma protested, almost losing her balance. 'I've already taken two tosses today without you pushing me over.'

'That's Destiny's way of telling you she likes you, Norma,' Mike chuckled. 'You've won.'

Norma smiled at him. 'Destiny won't let me down tomorrow,' she said. 'It will be up to me now to do my best for her.'

CHAPTER XVII

DESTINY'S DAY

There was a burst of clapping as Destiny successfully cleared the last fence of the difficult course for the Open Jumping Competition at the County Show next day.

'Number fifty-six had a clear round,' reported the loudspeaker.

Liz turned triumphantly to Toni. 'That means Norma will be in the jump-off.'

'So are Harkaway Boy, Deerfoot and Manny,' Pete pointed out. 'She's up against some stiff competition.'

'My money's on Norma,' Mike said from his wheel-chair.

Already the stewards were moving away the unwanted fences, leaving five for the shortened course over which the four competitors who had clear rounds would jump again to decide which would be the winner. The stewards left the in-and-out, the stile, the wall, the water jump and the triple bars. The wall and the triple were both raised.

'A tough and tricky course now,' said Mike.

His hands seemed tense on the big wheels of his chair as Harkaway Boy came into the ring.

The big bay jumped perfectly and had a second clear round. Then the rain began to fall. The Ponyways watchers huddled together under the macks that the few farsighted ones had brought, and made a canopy over Mike as the rain fell faster.

Deerfoot had four faults. Then Manny came into the ring. He was a lightly-built, springy chestnut. The top surface of the course was becoming muddy. Manny cleared the in-and-out, refused at the stile, took it eventually, knocked a brick off the wall, leapt the water jump, slipped as he turned for the triple bars and came down. He brought down all three bars. While the stewards were supervising the picking up of the jumps, Norma rode Destiny into the churned-up ring.

'If only the rain had held off!' Mike groaned, peering from under the canopy of mackintoshes.

Norma cantered Destiny to the in-and-out. The grey mare took it in her stride. She was playing to the gallery. Showily she cleared the stile, then the wall and the water jump. At the slippery corner where Manny had fallen, she almost came down, but recovered herself, put in a couple of quick strides and cleared the triple bars. Now she and Harkaway Boy would have to jump-off again.

This time the stewards left only two fences – the water jump and the wall which now looked over five feet.

Harkaway Boy cleared both with ease.

'Good luck, Norma,' breathed Liz as Destiny danced into the ring.

'This suspense is killing!' groaned Toni.

The mare also seemed to feel the electrifying excitement in the air. She reared in front of the grand-stand. Norma calmed her with a pat and a word. She swung the mare round and cantered her towards the water jump. With a sudden spurt of speed, they were over. Now for the wall. It was high for its width. Destiny could cover a wide spread with greater ease than she could jump an abrupt height.

'One, two, three – *up!*' Mike's lips moved as he willed Destiny to take off in time.

Almost as if she heard, Norma lifted Destiny to the jump. The mare's heels just touched the coping which rocked, but did not fall.

'Another jump-off!' Mike sighed. 'Poor Norma. I know just how she feels. It's nerve-racking.'

This time the jumps seemed frighteningly high.

Harkaway Boy pranced in, straining at his bit, lathering, eager to go. He plunged forward, went too fast at the water jump, knocked down the fence and landed in the water. Unsettled, he fretted up to the wall and jumped through it, scattering the 'bricks'.

'Now, it's up to you, Norma,' Liz murmured to herself.

A roar of applause came from the crowd as Destiny walked into the ring. The mare flicked her tail, almost nonchalantly trotting to the grand-stand end. Norma was half-blinded by the driving rain. She turned Destiny, and cantered her towards the water jump. Destiny skidded on the mud as she took off, recovered but landed in the water.

Liz groaned. A bad beginning! But Norma was checking

Destiny now, and giving her time to recover. A soothing pat on the neck and they were off again. Liz could imagine the tremendous power of Destiny, held almost tremblingly in check as Norma fought the mare's impatience. Suddenly Destiny rocketed ahead with tremendous impulse.

A gasp went up from the spectators as she hovered for a moment in mid-air. Then she was over the jump. The mare had only two faults to Harkaway Boy's four. Destiny had won.

'Cheers for Norma!' Toni exulted. 'One up to Ponyways. Oh, very good!'

'Bless you, Norma,' Mike said quietly, relaxed once more. 'Destiny's going to have a winning season after all.'

CHAPTER XVIII

PONYWAYS AT HOME

Soon after eleven o'clock next morning, Liz carried out coffee to the television engineers who were busy in front of Ponyways, running cables from their vans in readiness for the broadcast the following night.

Liz had just handed over the tray of cups when she caught sight of the Ponyways shooting-brake speeding up the drive with Norma at the wheel. Liz blinked. Could it be true? Sitting solidly at the back of the brake was Mrs Roylance.

'Oh, dear, I'm gettin' too fat for this thing!' panted the plump cook as she climbed out of the shooting-brake.

'Goodness, Mrs Roylance!' Liz ran to meet her. 'How lovely to see you!'

'An' to see you, dearie.' Mrs Roylance beamed. 'Mrs Dashmore came an' asked me so nice to come back, I could 'ardly refuse. Besides,' she confided proudly, 'the B.B.C. want me to be in the telly show.'

'Of course!' Norma put an arm round Mrs Roylance. 'You're part of Ponyways. The B.B.C. couldn't possibly have the programme without you, Mrs Roylance. I told the producer about you, and he said "Get her". Just like that. So I got you!'

Mrs Roylance chuckled. 'Think of it! Me! A star of the silver screen, as you might say! I bet some of them in the village won't 'arf get a shock when they switches their sets on tomorrow night. It'll put Ponyways proper in the picture, as you might say.' She broke off, and her expression changed. ''Course I was forgettin' young Robin. I only 'ope that he don't get sent to gaol when he comes up before the beak tomorrow. Proper blight on the proceedings that'd be!'

*

'Here, Pete!' Mike called from the landing next morning. 'I've been trying to get used to these crutches, but I can't manage the stairs. Just help me down, will you?'

'The shooting-brake's at the front door, Mike,' Norma called up. 'Mother's already in.' She saw Mike half-way down the stairs with his hand on Pete's shoulder. 'I was going to help you down, but I see Pete's beaten me to it.'

Just then Liz and Toni came into the hall.

'Mike's insisted on coming with Mummy and me to London this morning to rally round Robin in the police court,' Norma told them.

'What about the T.V. run-through?' Liz reminded her.

'Bruno says that it will be all right as long as we're back by four o'clock. Mrs Roylance and Maud will be getting lunch for everybody so that will give you a rest from the chores for a change.'

'Why not take the ponies on the Downs for a canter?' Mike suggested. 'They need exercise.'

'We'll do that,' said Liz.

As the shooting-brake moved off down the drive with Mike, Norma and Mrs Gill aboard, the other Ponyways guests, and Mrs Roylance and Maud, came out to wave, and to call good-luck messages.

'There's no luck around today,' Maud said forebodingly as the shooting-brake disappeared round the bend. 'It's only half past eight and I've already spilled salt, seen a crow – one for sorrow – and cracked the mirror in me 'and bag!'

'Seven years' bad luck!' For once Mrs Roylance seemed as gloomy as Maud. 'Nay! The beak couldn't give young Robin as long as that.'

'P'raps not.' Maud shook her head. 'But, you'll see,' she prophesied, in a voice of doom: 'when that shootin'-brake comes back up the drive this afternoon, Master Robin won't be in it!'

*

'Just as I said!' Maud craned mournfully out of the kitchen window as the Ponyways shooting-brake came up the drive soon after half past three that afternoon. 'They've all come back except Master Robin!'

The Jollison twins and Dave made a rush for the door, not able to restrain their eagerness to hear what had happened to Robin.

'Come back, you three!' Liz called quickly. 'Don't rush out. Stay here, and try not to look pop-eyed. Wait until Norma or Mike tell us what's happened, and for goodness' sake don't ask questions.'

The younger ones reluctantly dragged themselves away from the door, and Mrs Roylance waddled towards the stove.

'I'll put the kettle on. They'll be dropping!'

They heard Mrs Gill going upstairs, and Norma opening the garage doors. Mike's crutches tapped on the cobbles.

He stood in the doorway, looking round at the silent group.

'What a cathedral hush!' He smiled, and then looked apologetic. 'But, of course! You're all wondering what's happened to Robin. We ought to have telephoned you as soon as his case was over.'

Maud looked woeful.

'It's bad news, isn't it, Mister Mike?'

'Well, Robin was certainly found guilty —' Mike began.

'Seven years!' Maud gave a shriek. 'I knew it!'

'Don't be so soft, Maud,' Mrs Roylance told her sister. 'Seven months more like.'

'Not even seven weeks,' Mike said with a relieved smile. 'He's been put on probation for a year.'

Gerry's face fell.

'So he doesn't get locked up, after all!'

'No. He has to behave himself and report every week to the Probation Officer,' said Mike.

Mike sat down and Mrs Roylance handed him a cup of tea.

'But why hasn't young Robin come back with you?' she asked.

'Well, he had to stay because there were quite a lot of odds and ends that the Probation Officer wanted to look into,' Mike told them. 'He's got to decide where it would be best for Robin to live, and what sort of a job he should have.'

'Won't he be able to go on with his Rock 'n' Roll?' asked Dave.

'That's one of the things that the Probation Officer is looking into,' explained Mike.

'Poor Robin!' sighed Pete. 'Just as he's reached the top as a rocker he might have to give it all up, and sit on an office stool, being a "square" for the rest of his days!'

'Everybody ready?' the B.B.C. producer called from the hall a few moments later, and his engineers trundled their equipment behind him. 'Now relax, everybody ... Just be natural. We'll have a check-up before the final run-through.'

Meanwhile Mrs Roylance was bustling round the kitchen and sitting-room, trying to restore tidiness and polish up the furniture amid a welter of cameras, lights, wires and sound equipment.

'Hey, Ma, leave those cables alone, can't you?' begged a harassed sound engineer.

'You mind 'oo you're Maain',' Mrs Roylance said sharply, pushing him to one side with the polishing mop. 'I'd 'ave you know, young man, there wouldn't be no programme without me.'

The engineer grinned sardonically. 'And who might you be? Mrs Mop?'

'I'm the 'eart of Ponyways!' Mrs Roylance beamed proudly. 'At least that's what Mr Bruno Maxwell says. Proper nice gentleman, 'e is. Not that 'e wouldn't be better without them w'iskers, mind. But I dessay 'e's got to 'ave something, just to show 'e's important-like.'

She imparted a last flick of the mop to the underneath of the camera trolley and went back to the kitchen.

Out in the stables Liz was helping Norma to soothe Destiny

who had been startled almost out of her wits by the appearance of a camera and lighting equipment outside her loose-box door.

'We shall want a "live" shot of Destiny,' the B.B.C. producer insisted. 'After all she's the heroine of the hour. I thought we might fade-out, Norma, with you, Mike and Winton visiting her for a good-night pat.'

'That's a good idea,' Norma agreed. 'But how are we going to get Destiny to take it?'

'Put her in a different loose box,' Bruno suggested, 'while we rig hers up. Then we can get her used to it later, gradually.'

'Bribe her with apples,' suggested Liz who knew Destiny's weakness for a sweet, crunchy Beauty of Bath.

Time sped. Somehow Mrs Roylance and Maud managed to feed all the Ponyways inmates as well as the B.B.C. people.

Liz and Norma accustomed Destiny to the lights and camera in her loose box while Winton and Bruno rehearsed the interview with Mike, talked to the twins, Fay, Toni, Dave and Pete, and jotted down questions to ask them which might result in interesting or amusing replies.

Everything seemed to be going wonderfully except that Destiny would not face the cameras. Mike hobbled across from the house on his crutches, talked soothingly to the mare, gave her yet another apple, and coaxed her to follow him into the loose box.

'Fine!' Bruno approved. 'She'll do.'

'I hope you're right, Bruno.' Winton Blare backed nervously away from Destiny's hocks. 'If there's one thing I like less than a horse's teeth, it's his heels!'

The run-through went off without a hitch. Would they all be so lucky during the actual televising? Tension mounted. They were rehearsed, made-up, and dressed assortedly in jeans and jodhpurs. (Dave had refused to put on the Roy Rogers cowboy outfit which Bruno had wanted him to wear.) Now there was nothing to do but sit and wait for the programme to begin.

Mrs Gill came into the sitting-room.

'This place is like a bear-garden,' she complained. 'No

peace anywhere. I've had a headache all day. Three times I've fallen over trailing cables and might have broken my ankle.'

'Never mind, Mummy.' Norma patted the vacant place beside her on the sofa. 'Come and sit with us. We're all going to try to relax now, and watch the television programme on this monitor set until it's time for us to be on the air.'

When the set warmed up, the screen showed Warwick Dalziel, the well-known and breezy compère, in friendly close-up.

'Come with us and Hit the High Spots!' he invited. 'To-night we visit the Café du Continent, in London's West End. We open the show with a new young star. Ladies and gentlemen, presenting for the first time on television – Robin Rock, King of the Roll!'

'Good gracious!' said Mrs Gill.

'Hurrah!' the cheering at Ponyways drowned the clapping in the Café du Continent as Robin appeared on the screen, wearing gay check shirt and tight black jeans, confident and debonair as always.

'Sssh!' Mike signalled to the enthusiastic viewers. 'Let's hear the boy!'

Robin strolled to the microphone with his guitar.

'Listen, mister. Listen, sister.
Don't you knock the rock?'

To the accompaniment of frenzied drumming and trumpet-playing in the background, Robin leapt to galvanized activity. Plucking his guitar as he sang, and with his feet straddled in front of the microphone, he jerked and rocked in a crescendo of strumming and song.

'Robin's got something!' applauded Pete.

'I'll say,' Dave's feet beat automatically to the catchy rhythm.

'He's certainly no worse than any of the other crazy rock 'n' roll types they make such a fuss about,' said Cherry restrainedly.

Liz felt a surge of relief. Certainly Robin had made good this time. He had found the one thing he could do well. He had received a stern lesson from the law and perhaps that, coupled with his new-found ability to earn money honestly, would help him to go straight.

Robin's number came to a frenzied end, leaving several million viewers gasping.

Warwick Dalziel reappeared on the screen.

'Well, viewers, that was Robin Rock, the newly-crowned King of the Roll. Having seen his astounding performance you can understand why he has leapt to fame. Robin Rock is a new meteor who has shot to the dizzy heights. Robin Rock will be appearing nightly at the Café du Continent.'

Norma switched off the set as the compère went on to announce the next act.

'Good for Robin!' Mike said. 'The Probation Officer must have decided to let him rock 'n' roll after all.'

'How could even the law stand in Robin's way,' boomed Winton Blare, 'since a rock 'n' roll-crazy public will now make it possible for the boy to earn more than the Prime Minister?'

Mrs Gill's bewilderment turned to interest.

'Do you mean to say, Mr Blare, that my son will be well paid for this? How odd! Robin did say something about soon being in the "big money".' She looked round at everybody with pride. 'My son told me he would buy me a hat shop if he were allowed to rock 'n' roll.'

'Rest assured, dear lady,' Winton Blare said with bitter cynicism, 'such is the deplorable taste of the masses that – while true talent and real genius often go unrewarded – your son, in a very short time, will be the possessor of such wealth that he should be able to buy you a *chain* of hat shops.'

'One will do,' Mrs Gill said, sitting back contentedly. 'An exclusive shop, in some corner of Mayfair, to cater for the *élite*, of course.' She shut her eyes to visualize herself in such a plush setting. 'Yes, to run a hat shop these days is quite the U-thing to do.' She looked across at Norma and Mike. 'Of course I should have to take a flat in London. I couldn't possibly live here and travel back and forth.'

Mike and Norma somehow contrived to look regretful, and Liz, watching them, thought: '*Sic transit* Mrs Gill! Another Ponyways problem solved!'

'Three minutes to go, everybody,' the producer announced from the doorway. 'Take your place in the hall now, Mike, to be ready to meet Winton as he comes up the steps.' He spoke into a hand microphone. 'Is the sound O.K., Andy?'

'Sound O.K.,' came the reply into his headphones from an engineer in the sound van.

'Stand by!' said Bruno. 'We'll be on the air in twenty seconds from now ... Silence everybody. Come in when the red light flickers, Winton.'

A few moments later a steady light on Camera One proclaimed that Ponyways was on the air.

Winton Blare shook hands with Norma and Mike in the hall, and commiserated with Mike for being on crutches. Mike made light of this, welcomed the viewers to his home and introduced the sequence of film that had been taken of the jumping lessons and another sequence of Ponyways riders galloping over the Downs. Then Mike and Winton were shown entering the living-room.

'Now, these are some of the young riders at Ponyways, taking part in the holiday courses,' Winton said. He crossed over to Gerry. 'Were you in that film sequence we've just been looking at?'

'Yes, I was the one who fell off,' Gerry grinned.

'You're here with your twin brother, aren't you?' Winton asked. 'Have you been here before?'

'Twice,' said Gerry.

Winton turned to Toni. 'How many times have you been to Ponyways?'

'This is my second visit,' Toni smiled. 'I came with my cousin, Rosemary, and we arranged to come at the same time as Fay and Pete and Dave who we met last year.'

'I see.' Winton walked across to Liz, stood beside her, and said to the viewers: 'Now this young lady is a particular friend of mine. When some of the Ponyways horses bolted into my garden, she galloped after them—'

'And fell off into a barrow-load of your berberis prunings,' added Liz. 'But it was Mr Blare who captured the runaways.'

She told the viewers how Winton had resourcefully opened the stable door, and calmly shut it again when the horses had all cantered inside.

Just then, as arranged at the rehearsals, Mrs Roylance plumply waddled in, carrying a tray laden with mugs of cocoa.

'Ponyways' night-cap,' said Winton. 'This is the time of day when the young people settle down by the fire for a good yarn. They sing songs, too. Sometimes they have camp fires out of doors, with picnic suppers on the beach. We'll show you that in a minute, on a piece of film. In the meantime I want to introduce you to the most important person at any holiday establishment – the cook!'

'You've never spoken a truer word, sir.' Mrs Roylance folded her plump arms. 'A proper mix-up they all got into while I was away.'

'So I understand,' Winton Blare said weightily. 'That's the way it happens. As some wit once said: "She was a good cook as cooks go, and as good cooks go – she went!"'

'That's right.' Mrs Roylance joined in the laughter. 'I walked out as you might say, but I missed the children, ponies, dogs and all – so I walked back!'

'For always, I hope,' said Norma, coming into the picture and smiling from Mrs Roylance to Winton Blare. 'She's a treasure.'

Winton Blare faced the camera again. 'We now go from one important member of the Ponyways establishment to meet some more. On to the stables!'

The outside cameras took over as Mike, Norma and Winton Blare were shown coming out of the house and crossing the flood-lit courtyard.

In the sitting-room the Ponyways viewers craned to watch the monitor set which now showed Mike, on his crutches, moving to one side to let Norma lead the way into the main stable building.

The insides of the stables were lit-up, and, on the screen, the viewers could see horses' heads craning over the loose-box doors.

'This is Samba.' Norma introduced the tubby black pony and Winton gave him a lump of sugar.

'You're a grand fellow and a great friend of the younger Ponyways riders,' Winton told the black pony before moving on to the next loose box. 'Now who have we here?'

'He's already a friend of yours, Winton,' Norma said. 'This is Barney.'

After introducing the other ponies, the trio came to the last loose box and the cameras moved nearer to show Destiny in close-up.

'Meet Destiny,' Winton said as the camera angle changed and the humans were now shown again, this time grouped round Destiny. 'Mike Dashmore's famous show-jumping mare.'

Destiny gently took an apple from Winton. As her teeth crunched into the juicy sweetness a gleam of approval came into her eyes. She turned to Winton and bunted him in the chest, so that the portly celebrity staggered against the wall of the loose box.

'That's Destiny's favourite joke,' Mike told Winton. 'She does that only to people whom she likes.'

'I appreciate the honour,' said Winton, brushing the powdered white-wash off the wall from the back of his jacket. 'But I wish she had a less boisterous way of showing her friendliness.'

In the sitting-room at Ponyways, this unrehearsed side-light made the young guests chuckle. Liz leaned forward, her hands cupping her chin, hypnotized by the images on the screen.

The programme was going well. Norma was facing the camera, now telling the story of how Destiny had risen to the top flight in show-jumping. Mike had bought her as an unbroken mare. She told the viewers the mare had been five

years old and had never had a rider on her back. Many people would have felt she was too old to be properly broken-in and schooled. But not Mike. He had liked the look of Destiny and seen show-jumping possibilities in her powerful hocks and courageous look. Time had proved him right. Liz was held by Norma's quiet voice as she gave Mike all the credit for Destiny's training and for building up Ponyways as a holiday establishment for young riders.

Mike's and Norma's eyes met, and they smiled. Liz could see now how right they were for each other.

She felt herself flush with shame as she remembered how first Mrs Roylance, and then she and some of the other Ponyways guests, had felt that Norma was not good enough for Mike. She thought: 'In a way, we tried to come between husband and wife, and it was dreadful, of course — Dreadful! Suppose we'd succeeded ...? How glad I am that we failed.'

Liz stared at the monitor set.

Although Mike and Norma and life at Ponyways was reduced to black-and-white, on a 17-inch screen, it seemed to Liz that she was seeing things more clearly than ever before.

'Norma knew we all resented her ... Perhaps she still feels we do,' Liz thought. 'We must show her that we like her. We must convince her. But how?'

Liz sat back as Winton brought the programme to an end. Behind his voice crept the music of a violin, a flute and an oboe playing *Greensleeves*.

A few minutes later, the sitting-room door opened, and Norma stood on the threshold with Mike. He had discarded one crutch, and she was supporting him with her right arm round his waist.

There was a trace of anxiety in her glance as she looked round at the Ponyways household.

'Well, how did it come over?'

'You were both a treat,' said Mrs Roylance wiping her eyes on the corner of her apron.

'Splendid, Norma, dear,' approved Mrs Gill.

'Whizz!' said Gerry.

'Super!' added George.

'You and Mike weren't a bit camera shy!' said Toni.

'Wasn't it terrific when Destiny bunted Winton Blare?' chuckled Dave.

As all the others gave their opinions, Liz tried to think of words to express her feelings, to say something that would convince Norma that they all liked her as much as they liked Mike. She felt Norma's eyes on her doubtfully, wondering what she was thinking.

Liz stood up, her eyes shining behind her spectacles.

She stretched out a hand to Norma, took a deep breath and impulsively burst into song.

'For she's a jolly good fellow!'

'And so say all of us!' chorused the others while Candy and Floss barked in agreement.

Even Maud, standing spectre-like by the window with her plump sister, for once was unable to make a gloomy prognostication.

'Mark my words, Em,' she told Mrs Roylance. 'This 'ere programme's done somethink for Ponyways. It's turned us all into one 'appy family. Things is goin' to be luverly from now on!'